NAVAL
POSTGRADUATE
SCHOOL

MONTEREY, CALIFORNIA

THESIS

COALITION SPACE OPERATIONS: EXPLORING NEW PATHS FOR ALLIED PARTNERSHIP

by

Robert H. Manuel

June 2018

Thesis Advisor:	James C. Moltz
Second Reader:	Alan D. Scott

Approved for public release. Distribution is unlimited.

THIS PAGE INTENTIONALLY LEFT BLANK

REPORT DOCUMENTATION PAGE			Form Approved OMB No. 0704-0188
Public reporting burden for this collection of information is estimated to average 1 hour per response, including the time for reviewing instruction, searching existing data sources, gathering and maintaining the data needed, and completing and reviewing the collection of information. Send comments regarding this burden estimate or any other aspect of this collection of information, including suggestions for reducing this burden, to Washington headquarters Services, Directorate for Information Operations and Reports, 1215 Jefferson Davis Highway, Suite 1204, Arlington, VA 22202-4302, and to the Office of Management and Budget, Paperwork Reduction Project (0704-0188) Washington, DC 20503.			
1. AGENCY USE ONLY *(Leave blank)*	**2. REPORT DATE** June 2018	**3. REPORT TYPE AND DATES COVERED** Master's thesis	
4. TITLE AND SUBTITLE COALITION SPACE OPERATIONS: EXPLORING NEW PATHS FOR ALLIED PARTNERSHIP			**5. FUNDING NUMBERS**
6. AUTHOR(S) Robert H. Manuel			
7. PERFORMING ORGANIZATION NAME(S) AND ADDRESS(ES) Naval Postgraduate School Monterey, CA 93943-5000			**8. PERFORMING ORGANIZATION REPORT NUMBER**
9. SPONSORING / MONITORING AGENCY NAME(S) AND ADDRESS(ES) N/A			**10. SPONSORING / MONITORING AGENCY REPORT NUMBER**
11. SUPPLEMENTARY NOTES The views expressed in this thesis are those of the author and do not reflect the official policy or position of the Department of Defense or the U.S. Government.			
12a. DISTRIBUTION / AVAILABILITY STATEMENT Approved for public release. Distribution is unlimited.			**12b. DISTRIBUTION CODE** A

13. ABSTRACT (maximum 200 words)

The use of satellites to support military operations has grown dramatically in recent years, which has increased the exposure of military satellite systems to targeting. To combat this risk to its space systems, the Department of Defense has prescribed increased military space cooperation with the United States' closest friends and allies. This thesis investigates the United States' history of partnering with three of its closest allies—France, Australia, and Japan—since the dawn of the space age to see where the best opportunities for enhanced military space cooperation exist today. It finds that changes in the military space organizations, capabilities, and policies of these three allies since 2008 have significantly increased the ability of their militaries to collaborate fruitfully with the Department of Defense. Furthermore, aided by the ongoing growth of their military space cadres, collaboration with these countries can expand from a traditional focus on technical applications into combined education, doctrine, and policy. The thesis closes on a cautionary note, arguing that the Department of Defense needs to carefully consider how it will develop trust with foreign spacefaring militaries, with the Department of Commerce likely to assume responsibility for the foreign engagement associated with the United States' space situational awareness data-sharing agreements by 2024.

14. SUBJECT TERMS France, Australia, Japan, national, security, space, strategy, international, cooperation, cooperate, collaboration, collaborate, military, coalition, allies, Ally, SATCOM, ISR, PNT, defense, satellite, launch, policy, SSA, engagement, awareness, disaggregate			**15. NUMBER OF PAGES** 123
			16. PRICE CODE
17. SECURITY CLASSIFICATION OF REPORT Unclassified	**18. SECURITY CLASSIFICATION OF THIS PAGE** Unclassified	**19. SECURITY CLASSIFICATION OF ABSTRACT** Unclassified	**20. LIMITATION OF ABSTRACT** UU

NSN 7540-01-280-5500

Standard Form 298 (Rev. 2-89)
Prescribed by ANSI Std. 239-18

THIS PAGE INTENTIONALLY LEFT BLANK

COALITION SPACE OPERATIONS: EXPLORING NEW PATHS FOR ALLIED PARTNERSHIP

Robert H. Manuel
Major, United States Marine Corps
BA, Clemson University, 2003

Submitted in partial fulfillment of the
requirements for the degree of

MASTER OF SCIENCE IN SPACE SYSTEMS OPERATIONS

from the

NAVAL POSTGRADUATE SCHOOL
June 2018

Approved by: James C. Moltz
                 Advisor

                 Alan D. Scott
                 Second Reader

                 James H. Newman
                 Chair, Department of Space Systems Academic Group

iii

THIS PAGE INTENTIONALLY LEFT BLANK

ABSTRACT

The use of satellites to support military operations has grown dramatically in recent years, which has increased the exposure of military satellite systems to targeting. To combat this risk to its space systems, the Department of Defense has prescribed increased military space cooperation with the United States' closest friends and allies. This thesis investigates the United States' history of partnering with three of its closest allies—France, Australia, and Japan—since the dawn of the space age to see where the best opportunities for enhanced military space cooperation exist today. It finds that changes in the military space organizations, capabilities, and policies of these three allies since 2008 have significantly increased the ability of their militaries to collaborate fruitfully with the Department of Defense. Furthermore, aided by the ongoing growth of their military space cadres, collaboration with these countries can expand from a traditional focus on technical applications into combined education, doctrine, and policy. The thesis closes on a cautionary note, arguing that the Department of Defense needs to carefully consider how it will develop trust with foreign spacefaring militaries, with the Department of Commerce likely to assume responsibility for the foreign engagement associated with the United States' space situational awareness data-sharing agreements by 2024.

THIS PAGE INTENTIONALLY LEFT BLANK

TABLE OF CONTENTS

LIST OF ACRONYMS AND ABBREVIATIONS

ANZUS	Australia, New Zealand, and the United States
Athena-Fidus	Access on Theatres and European Nations for Allied Forces - French Italian Dual Use Satellite
CERES	Capacité de Renseignement Électromagnétique Spatiale
CIE	Commandement Interarmées de l'Espace
CNES	Centre National d'Etudes Spatiales
CSIRO	Commonwealth Scientific and Industrial Research Organization
CSpO	Combined Space Operations
Comsat	Communications Satellite Corporation
COSMO-SkyMed	Constellation of Small Satellite for the Mediterranean Basin Observation-SkyMed
CSO	Composante Spatiale Optique
DoD	Department of Defense
DSP	Defense Satellite Program
EHF	Extremely High Frequency
ELDO	European Launcher Development Organization
ELINT	Electronic Intelligence
ELISA	Electronic Intelligence Satellite
ESA	European Space Agency
EU	European Union
EUMETSAT	European Organisation for the Exploitation of Meteorological Satellites
FEDOME	Fédération des Données de Météorologie de l'Espace
GDP	Gross Domestic Product
GPS	Global Positioning System
GRAVES	Grand Réseau Adapté à la Veille Spatiale
IC	intelligence community
ICBM	Intercontinental Ballistic Missile
IGS	Information Gathering Satellites
Intelsat	International Telecommunications Satellite Organization

ISCS	International Space Cooperation Strategy
ITAR	International Trafficking in Arms Regulations
JAXA	Japan Aerospace Exploration Agency
JSDF	Japan Self-Defense Forces
LPM	Loi de Programmation Militaire
MUSIS	Multinational Space-based Imaging System
Oscegeane	Observation Spectrale et Caractérisation des Satellites Géostationnaires
NASA	National Aeronautics and Space Administration
NASDA	National Aeronautics and Space Development Agency
NATO	North Atlantic Treaty Organization
OSCAR	Orbiting Satellite Carrying Amateur Radio
PNT	position, navigation, and timing
SAR-Lupe	Synthetic Aperture Radar-Lupe
SATAM	Système d'Acquisition et de Trajectographie des Avions et des Munitions
SATCOM	satellite communication
SBIRS	Space-Based Infrared System
Sicral	Sistema Italiano per Comunicazioni Riservate ed Allarmi
SHF	Super High Frequency
SPARTA	Special Antimissile Research Tests, Australia
Spirale	Système Préparatoire Infra-Rouge pour l'Alerte
SPOT	Système Probatoire d'Observation de la Terre
SSA	Space Situational Awareness
Syracuse	Systeme de Radio Communications Utilisant un Satellite
TAROT	Télescope à Action Rapide pour les Objets Transitoires
UHF	Ultra High Frequency
UN	United Nations
WGS	Wideband Global SATCOM

ACKNOWLEDGMENTS

Special thanks go to James C. Moltz, a consummate thesis advisor.

THIS PAGE INTENTIONALLY LEFT BLANK

I.   INTRODUCTION

In 2010, the United States pivoted toward increased international collaboration in space under the Obama administration. Partnering with responsible nations in space was a key tenet of the 2011 National Security Space Strategy.[1] Increased partnering with responsible nations took on a number of forms during the administration, to include reforms to International Trafficking in Arms Regulations and the signing of space situational sharing agreements with a total of 63 commercial partners, multi-lateral organizations, and countries by early 2016.[2] In addition to these two efforts, the incorporation of Canada, the United Kingdom, Australia, and New Zealand into the Combined Space Operations initiative with the United States represented a significant nascent effort to create coalition operations in space. Moving toward the current administration, the U.S. Department of Defense sought to bring other like-minded allies and partners, such as Japan, France, and Germany, into the Combined Space Operations initiative.

The fundamental question this thesis seeks to answer is, "How might the United States benefit from coalition operations in space?" While determining how the United States can benefit from coalition operations in space with all like-minded countries is beyond the scope of this work, the thesis takes on the more modest task of a case study approach to examine how the United States can benefit from coalition operations in space with three countries—Australia, France, and Japan.

Studying this particular set of countries is warranted for several reasons. First, each country has long-standing security agreements with the United States, but each agreement is different. As such, each agreement has unique benefits and drawbacks when it comes to cooperation. For example, Australia is a "Five-Eye" country, which facilitates the sharing

---

[1] Defense Department and Office of the Director of National Intelligence, *National Security Space Strategy (Unclassified Summary)* (Washington, DC: U.S. Department of Defense, January 2011), http://archive.defense.gov/ home/features/2011/0111_nsss/, 5.

[2] *Fiscal Year 2017 Budget Request for National Security Space: Hearing before the Armed Services Committee*, House, 114th Cong., 2nd sess. (March 15, 2016) (statement of Doug Loverro, Deputy Assistant Secretary of Defense for Space Policy, Department of Defense), 10.

of intelligence, but not a NATO ally, which does more to facilitate collaboration in research and development.

Second, each country maintains significant space capabilities of its own, capabilities that can increase the United States' mission capability and resilience capacity when operating as a coalition force. In this regard, Australia can be seen as somewhat lacking: Unlike Japan and France, Australia has never developed an independent launch capability. Of the "Five-Eye" countries covered by the UK-USA agreement, however, Australia and the United States have collaborated the most actively in defense related space in recent years. In 2013 and 2014, for example, the United States and Australia entered into agreements to relocate tracking radars to Australia to better monitor space activities in the southern hemisphere.[3] Similarly, France is a more interesting case than Germany because of France's early and sustained involvement in military-to-military cooperation in the Helios-II satellite program and because it is arguably the leading voice concerning space politics in Europe.

Third, each country has a unique political situation constraining the interaction and cooperation it can enter into with the United States. This is clearly exemplified by Japan, whose Basic Space Law forbade it from conducting military operations in space prior to the law's revision in 2008. Not until 2015, then, did Japan and the United States sign The Guidelines for Japan-U.S. Defense Cooperation, which pledged closer military cooperation with the United States Department of Defense across a broad spectrum of space mission areas.[4]

A.   SIGNIFICANCE OF THE RESEARCH QUESTION

The 2011 U.S. National Security Space Strategy reflects changes in U.S. government thinking about space that continue even today. Recent government analysis of space security posits that the strategic environment of space has become "congested, contested, and competitive" and that a host of conditions threatens the ability of the

---

[3] H., Fiscal Year 2017 Budget Request, 4–5.

[4] Japanese Ministry of Defense, *The Guidelines for Japan-U.S. Defense Cooperation*, April 27, 2015, http://www.mod.go.jp/e/d_act/anpo/shishin_20150427e.html.

Department of Defense's satellite constellations to accomplish their mission in support of the joint force. The Obama Administration set forth increasing the "interoperability, compatibility, and integration of partner nations into appropriate DoD and IC networks" as a strategy to mitigate some of these threats to mission accomplishment.[5] While the United States has yet to establish all of the conditions necessary to conduct coalition operations in space, nearly twenty years of thinking about the strategic imperatives of space has led it to pursue coalition operations in space as a policy objective.

The path toward the first ever National Security Space Strategy began in 1999 when the Fiscal Year 2000 National Defense Authorization Act mandated the creation of a commission to assess the management and organization of the U.S. national security space activities.[6] The so-called "Space Commission" that resulted from the authorization act found, in early 2001, that the United States critically needed to elevate space on the national security agenda.[7] Concerns that would later animate the Bush administration's approach to space security were manifest in the report, to include the ability of space to "speed the transformation of the U.S. military into a modern force," the need to shape the regulatory environment to ensure U.S. national security interests, and the recognition among potential adversaries that U.S. space assets made attractive targets.[8] The commission identified five matters of key importance as needing the government's quick attention, two of which would directly impact the development of a national security space strategy. The commission cited the need for "specific guidance and direction from the very highest government levels … to ensure the United States remains the world's leading space fairing nation."[9] It further recognized that the Secretary of Defense and the Director of Central

---

[5] Defense Department and Office of the Director of National Intelligence, *National Security Space Strategy*, 9.

[6] *National Defense Authorization Act for Fiscal Year 2000*, Public Law 106–65, 106th Cong., 1st sess., January 6, 1999.

[7] Commission to Assess U.S. National Security Space Management and Organization, *Report of the Commission to Assess U.S. National Security Space Management and Organization*, January 11, 2001, https://fas.org/spp/military/commission/report.htm.

[8] Commission to Assess, *Report of the Commission,* 5–7. See the *2002 Annual Defense Report* and the *2006 U.S. National Space Policy* for repetition of these themes during the Bush administration.

[9] Commission to Assess, *Report of the Commission,* 9–10.

Intelligence as the two officials primarily responsible for national space programs. In succeeding the Director of Central Intelligence as the head of the U.S. intelligence community, as a consequence of the Intelligence Reform and Intelligence Prevention Act of 2004, the Director of National Intelligence later assumed overall responsibility for the intelligence community's space programs as well.[10]

In 2003, the Government Accountability Office recommended specifically that the Department of Defense develop a national security space strategy and plan that would enable it to achieve the goals that the 1996 national space policy established for the department.[11] In 2008, the Government Accountability Office sent a follow-up letter to the Senate, explaining that the development of a legitimate national security space strategy would require closer collaboration between the intelligence community and the Department of Defense than anticipated in 2001, while it further stated that "cultural differences" between the intelligence and defense communities was making collaboration on such a document difficult.[12] As a result, the Government Accountability Office recommended that Congress require the Secretary of Defense and the Director of National Intelligence to work together to develop and issue a National Security Space Strategy.

The collaborative effort of the Secretary of Defense and the Director of National Intelligence manifested itself in the first ever National Security Space Strategy in 2011. This document flows from the United States Space Policy issued in 2010, which places greater emphasis on the shared and international use of space more than previous national space policies had. The 2011 National Security Space Strategy expresses a preoccupation with a strategic space environment that had become "congested, contested, and competitive."

---

[10] Office of the Director of National Intelligence, "ODNI Factsheet," February 24, 2017, 1, https://www.dni.gov/files/documents/FACTSHEET_ODNI_History_and_Background_2_24-17.pdf.

[11] Government Accountability Office, Defense Space Activities: *Organizational Changes Initiated but Further Management Actions Needed*, GAO-03-379, April 18, 2003, https://www.gao.gov/new.items/d03379.pdf.

[12] Government Accountability Office, "Letter to the Chairman and Ranking Member of the United States Committee on Armed Services," Subcommittee on Strategic forces dated March 27, 2008, GAO-08-431R, https://www.gao.gov/new.items/d08431r.pdf.

The relatively congested space environment of 2011 and today has resulted from a sharp increase in space debris in recent years. Since the dawn of the space age, the number of spacefaring nations has increased linearly at a rate of about one nation per year. Meanwhile, space debris 10 cm in diameter or larger has increased exponentially from zero objects in 1957, to 5,000 objects in 1982, and to approximately 23,000 objects currently.[13] The Chinese government's use of an anti-satellite weapon to destroy one of its own aging, on-orbit weather satellites in 2007 and the collision of an Iridium telecommunications satellite with a retired Russian military communications satellite in 2009 contributed significantly to the recent increase in space debris. If space debris continues to increase exponentially, it could crowd satellites out of affected orbits in the near future.

While the space environment has become more congested, countries have quickly developed an interest in technologies that would allow them to contest operations within the space environment as well. This has followed from the United States use of space to conduct military operations. From the 1991 Gulf War to Operation Enduring Freedom, space operations transitioned from strategic-level integration down to tactical-level integration into U.S. military operations.[14] Precision navigation and timing, satellite communications, space imagery, space weather, and overhead persistent reconnaissance have all assumed a direct support role in combat. According to Doug Loverro, Assistant Undersecretary of Defense for Space Policy for the Obama Administration, testifying before the House Armed Services Committee in 2016: "Chinese military strategists began writing about the targeting of space assets as a 'tempting and most irresistible choice' in the late 1990s, and the People's Liberation Army has been pursuing the necessary capabilities ever since."[15] Unlike the destructive measures employed by China during its anti-satellite attack demonstration in 2007, nations or individuals can assemble the technology required to jam satellites fairly easily. Given the asymmetric advantage that

---

[13] Defense Department and Office of the Director of National Intelligence, *National Security Space Strategy*, 1–2. See also J. C. Liou, "Growth of Orbital Debris," 4th ASEAN Regional Forum (ARF) Workshop on Space Security, October 24–25, 2016, https://ntrs.nasa.gov/archive/nasa/casi.ntrs.nasa.gov/20160012733.pdf.

[14] Pawlikowski et al., "Space: Disruptive Challenges," 32–33.

[15] H., *Fiscal Year 2017 Budget Request*, 5.

space provides to U.S. military forces and the ability of adversaries to target space assets for destruction or degradation, space has become a contested environment for the United States.

Marking an increasingly competitive environment, the U.S. share of worldwide revenue from satellite manufacturing fell from 67 percent in 1997 to 41 percent in 2007.[16] The U.S. portion of global satellite industry revenues then stabilized at about 43 percent of the world total over the following seven years.[17] Restrictive U.S. export control laws led foreign suppliers of space technology to market their products as "ITAR free" during this same period.[18] Meanwhile, second- and third-tier suppliers in the United States found themselves severely challenged by U.S. market conditions.[19] Recognizing the ongoing challenge to U.S. satellite manufacturers, the Trump administration's current National Security Strategy lists simplifying and updating regulations to strengthen the competitiveness of U.S. firms on the global market as a priority action.[20]

As the strategic environment has become more challenging, the U.S. Department of Defense acquisition system has begun to face challenges of its own in the development and procurement of space technologies. During the Cold War, satellites were strategic and highly classified.[21] While important, the cost of U.S. satellites was given less weight than it is today. Individual satellites tended to be smaller and cost less, and they were expected to last only three to five years on orbit. This created a regular demand signal for the satellite technology industry and a healthy supply chain.

---

[16] Defense Department and Office of the Director of National Intelligence, *National Security Space Strategy*, 3.

[17] The Tauri Group, "State of the Satellite Industry Report," prepared for the Satellite Industry Association, September 2015, https://www.sia.org/wp-content/uploads/2015/06/Mktg15-SSIR-2015-FINAL-Compressed.pdf.

[18] Joan Johnson-Freese, *Space as a Strategic Asset* (New York: Columbia University Press, 2007), 49.

[19] Defense Department and Office of the Director of National Intelligence, *National Security Space Strategy*, 3.

[20] Office of the President of the United States, *National Security Strategy of the United States of America* (December 2017), 31.

[21] Pawlikowski et al., "Space: Disruptive Challenges," 31–32.

In the 1990s, the growing competitiveness of foreign manufacturers of space technologies coincided with less spending on space technologies after the end of the Cold War.[22] Already challenging market conditions were exacerbated by improved satellite reliability, reducing the demand for parts. Tough market conditions led to the consolidation of the U.S. satellite industry under prime, first-tier suppliers. Cost and delivery times began to swell as industrial competitiveness waned. Similarly, launch costs increased, and the launch base became less flexible. The United States began to field fewer but larger, more capable satellites. The end result has left the U.S. government with a more vulnerable set of constellations than it had in the more permissible space environment of the late years of the Cold War.

The recent testimony and interviews of such leading governmental space authorities as Stephen Kitay, Deputy Assistant Secretary of Defense for Space Policy in the Trump administration, and Doug Loverro, his predecessor in the Obama administration, provide insight into the benefits and challenges of coalition operations in space today. In a December 2017 interview with *Space News*, Kitay postulated a current need to work with international partners to develop and rules of engagement and international norms of behavior for space.[23] In testimony before Congress in 2014 and 2016, respectively, Loverro argued for the ability of coalition operations to provide for resilience, and thereby mission assurance, as well as to complicate the strategic calculus of potential adversaries in space.[24][25] One of the ways that coalition space operations complicates the strategic calculus of the of the U.S. military's potential adversaries is by disaggregating space capabilities onto multiple systems.[26] Attacking coalition space assets multiplies the diplomatic repercussions for the potential adversaries as well.

---

[22] Pawlikowski et al., "Space: Disruptive Challenges," 31–34.

[23] Sandra Erwin, "DoD Space Policy Chief: 'It's imperative that we innovate,'" *Space News*, December 4, 2017, http://spacenews.com/dod-space-policy-chief-its-imperative-that-we-innovate/.

[24] *Fiscal Year 2015 and Future Years Defense Program, Committee on Armed Service, Subcommittee on Strategic Forces*, 13th Cong., 2nd sess., (March 12, 2014) (statement of Doug Loverro, Deputy Assistant Secretary of Defense for Space Policy, Department of Defense), 6–7.

[25] H., *Fiscal Year 2017 Budget Request*, 9.

[26] Air Force Space Command, "Resiliency and Disaggregated Space Architectures," August 21, 2013, 1, http://www.afspc.af.mil/Portals/3/documents/AFD-130821-034.pdf?ver=2016-04-14-154819-347.

In summary, the Office of the Director of National Intelligence and the Department of Defense developed the 2011 National Security Space Strategy because Congress had recognized that the use of space had become an increasingly vital and challenged element of national power. The National Security Space Strategy characterized space as a "congested, contested, and competitive" environment at the time of its release. Furthermore, it prescribed increased partnering with allies as a strategy to protect the security of the United States in this challenging space environment. This thesis addresses the research question, "How might the United States benefit from coalition operations in space?" so that the United States may implement its National Security Space Strategy more fully and one day operate as a coalition force in space.

B.   LITERATURE REVIEW

Surveying literature written on the subject of space security since 2001, there are two discernable points of inflection. The idea of space control was ascendant in the United States until 2007–2008. International criticism on moral and practical grounds saw literature on space control overcome by literature advocating for more collective approaches to space security, such as the space deterrence strategy set forth by the Obama administration, at that time. Space deterrence then began to face its own political challenges in 2013, leading to increased criticism of the Obama administration's deterrence strategy starting in 2015–2016. Authors have tended to criticize the U.S. deterrence strategy for space on methodological grounds rather than moral grounds since then.

Everett Dolman's book *Astropolitik* received a number of positive reviews following its publication in 2001.[27] Dolman espoused the idea that a major power would inevitably establish military control of space in order to set the laws and conditions for the exploitation of space resources. He argued that this would be the United States, by dent of its moral legitimacy as a great liberal democratic power. This space hegemon would then use the bounty gained from its early exploitation of space to maintain its supremacy and

---

[27] See John B. Sheldon, "Astropolitik: Classical Geopolitics in the Space Age," *Comparative Strategy*, vol. 21, no. 3 (2002), 235–237 and Peter Hays, "The Military Use of Space: A diagnostic Assessment / On the Edge of ...," *Air and Space Power Journal*, vol. 16, no. 3 (Fall 2002), 103–104 for positive receptions of the book.

benevolently rule the rest of the world in space.[28] Corollaries to Dolman's work could be found in the writing of John J. Klein, as well as in the preoccupation with space-power theory evidenced by, among others, Peter Hays.[29]

Fraser MacDonald's 2007 article "Anti-Astropolitik – outer space and the orbit of geography" is fairly representative of the international community's response to Astropolitik. Among his other criticisms, MacDonald wrote that Dolman's "sunny view that the United States is 'willing to extend legal and political equality to all' sits awkwardly with the current suspension of the rule of law in Guantanamo Bay as well as in various other 'spaces of exception.'"[30] Joan Johnson-Freese criticized Dolman's work indirectly in *Space as a Strategic Asset* in her critique of the Bush-era space policy of the United States. She took issue with the Bush administration's efforts to control the spread of space technology that it was, in fact, unable to control and with its policies that tended to advocate for the weaponization of outer space, at least by the United States.[31]

Along with others, James Clay Moltz found himself at an inflection point in the space policy debate in 2008 when he wrote: "A key question that will affect space security is whether states will fall back on self-absorbed nationalist approaches—as has so frequently occurred in the past—or whether they will be willing to accept the inevitable transaction costs of collective security approaches. One possibility is that, coalitions or even alliances might form in space."[32] The Obama administration helped usher in a collective security approach with its National Security Strategy in 2010 and its National Security Space Strategy in 2011. Closer security relations with friends and allies was but

---

[28] Everett C. Dolman, *Astropolitik: Classical Geopolitics in the Space Age* (London: Frank Cass, 2002), 181.

[29] See John J. Klein, *Space Warfare: Strategy, Principles, and Policy* (New York: Routledge, 2006) and Charles D. Lutes and Peter Hays, *Toward a Theory of Spacepower: Selected Essays*, (Washington, DC: National Defense University, 2011).

[30] Fraser MacDonald, "Anti-Astropolitik – Outer Space and the Orbit of Geography," *Progress in Human Geography*, vol. 31, no. 5, 2007, 608.

[31] Johnson-Freese, *Space as a Strategic Asset*.

[32] James Clay Moltz, "Next Steps towards Space Security," in *Space Security*, ed. Sukhvinder Kaur Multani (India: The Ifcai University Press, 2008).

one part of the United States space strategy, aimed primarily at deterrence rather than at space control.

In 2011, Moltz again wrote about the potential for coalition operations in space, this time discussing their ability to usher in international norms and provide resilience for the United States and its closest friends and allies.[33] Dovetailing off of Moltz's work, Al Scott built upon the idea that lack of familiarity with allied and friendly space capabilities has prevented closer collaboration between militaries in the areas of Space Situational Awareness and Intelligence, Surveillance, and Reconnaissance.[34] This literature saw international progress as elusive, in 2011 even, and presented greater knowledge of foreign capabilities in defense-related space activities as part of the solution.

In a 2016 work, Paul Meyer calls for de-escalatory commentary on space developments as well as some well-publicized commentary on exercises in transparency in the wake of several failed efforts to create international legislature on space activities in 2013.[35] In 2016, Theresa Hitchens and Joan Johnson-Freese also cite 2013 as the year that the United States moved away from a policy of strategic restraint, following suspicious Chinese tests near the altitude required to maintain geostationary orbit.[36] Hitchens and Johnson-Freese call for a greater emphasis on "positive deterrence" in the next United States National Security Space Strategy, explaining that "positive deterrence includes taking into account the interests of potential adversaries and seeking to mitigate threat perceptions of one's own actions and intentions."[37]

---

[33] James Clay Moltz, "Coalitions in Space: Where Networks Are Power," *Space and Defense*, vol. 5, no. 1 (Summer 2011), 5–22.

[34] Alan D. Scott, "Coalition Building in Space: Initial Technical Considerations and Potential Implementation Strategies." [Prepared as a supplement to the Defense Threat Reduction Agency's project on "Allied Security and an Integrated Satellite Network"] (August 2011), 1.

[35] Paul Meyer, "Dark Forces Awaken: the Prospects for Cooperative Space Security," *The Nonproliferation Review*, vol. 23, nos. 3–4 (June-July 2016), 495–503, DOI: 10.1080/10736700.2016. 1268750.

[36] Theresa Hitchens and Joan Johnson-Freese, "Toward a New National Security Strategy: Time for Strategic Rebalancing," Atlantic Council Strategy Paper No. 5, *Atlantic Council* (June 2016), iii.

[37] Hitchens and Johnson-Freese, "Toward a New," *Atlantic Council*, 27–28.

Interestingly, while Hitchens and Johnson-Freese critique the U.S. strategy of deterrence generally and mention the expressed desire of Obama administration to increase allied cooperation specifically, their discussion of the subject of allied cooperation is largely divorced from the larger argument for positive deterrence. The same can be said for a critique that Christopher Stone makes of the National Security Space Strategy, in 2015, in which he explains that the U.S. deterrence strategy lacks a contextual understanding of the historical and cultural realities of the post-Cold War security environment.[38] Thus, these two authors criticized the method in which the United States went about its deterrence strategy up through 2016 without engaging critically how the United States pursued allied cooperation in space.

C.   POTENTIAL EXPLANATIONS AND HYPOTHESES

As presented in the opening paragraph of this thesis, the United States has made modest progress in the creation of space coalition in the last several years. If progress is to continue in building a space coalition, however, and especially if it is going to expand to new partners, such as France and Japan, the United States must critically consider the barriers to such coalition operations and how to overcome them. Similar to efforts at getting the intelligence community and the Department of Defense to collaborate on a National Security Space Strategy in the 2000s, efforts at creating a coalition space network have "cultural differences" to overcome. Specifically, experts have commonly cited a lack of firm political leadership, realistic milestones, adequate technological capabilities, and trust in handling sensitive information as barriers to meaningful coalition operations in space.[39]

The answers to two questions will likely inform the operations of any successful space coalition including France, Australia, or Japan and the United States. First, how does military space in each country work? Second, how might the militaries of each country work together as a space coalition force? The current discussion in the United States on coalition building in space has given inadequate attention to these two methodological

---

[38] Christopher Stone, "Security through Vulnerability? The False Deterrence of the National Security Space Strategy," *The Space Review*, April 13, 2015, http://www.thespacereview.com/article/2731/1.

[39] Jana Robinson, "Space Security through the Transatlantic Partnership," *Space Policy* No. 28, February 1, 2012, 61–62.

11

questions, especially if we extend the relevant topics beyond technological capabilities to include information germane to political leadership, realistic milestones, and trust in handling sensitive space-related data. This lacuna may be filled, in part, by incorporating the arguments that well-respected foreign authors have made about the inner workings of space-related defense efforts in their own countries more fully than past literature has done.

In 2010, for example, American and British authors Saadia M. Pekkanen and Paul Kallender-Umezu made a seemingly convincing argument about the increased and ongoing militarization of Japanese space programs. They argued that setbacks in the Japanese commercial space industry had led corporations to push their allies in the Japanese government toward military space projects, with attendant changes in the country's formal laws, institutions, plans, and policies.[40] In a review of the book, Japanese space policy advisor and professor at Hokkaido University Kazuto Suzuki wrote that "although their argument seems to coherently explain the history of Japanese space policy, it is not only unconvincing but also misleading for readers, who may not know enough about Japanese space policy." Suzuki referred to his own extensive research on space policy, going back eight years, to support this argument in the review. Being Japanese does not make Suzuki inherently right about any aspect of space-defense in Japan, but an author with his credentials and experience in space policy ought to be included in a scholarly thesis about Japanese space programs.

Frenchmen Francois Heisbourg and Xavier Pasco propose in Military Space: Europe between Sovereignty and Cooperation that their work is the first to treat in a systematic manner European cooperation in military space.[41] As a unique example of international military collaboration in electro-optical satellites, the *Helios* satellites figure prominently in Heisbourg and Pasco's presentation of lesson learned.[42] The challenges

---

[40] Saadia M. Pekkanen and Paul Kallender-Umezu, *In Defense of Japan: From the Market to the Military in Space Policy* (Stanford, CA: Stanford University Press, 2010), 2.

[41] Francois Heisbourg and Xavier Pasco, *Espace Militaire: L'Europe entre souveraineté et cooperation* (Paris: Choiseul, 2011), 11.

[42] Alain Claverie, Jean-Piere Darnis, et al. "Towards disruptions in Earth observation? New Earth Observation systems and markets evolution: Possible scenarios and impacts." *Acta Astronautica* No. 137 (2017), 418.

faced by France, Germany, Italy, Spain, and others in the course of the *Helios* programs aligns with the corporate knowledge as to what makes collaboration in space difficult, especially for the military. Heisbourg and Pasco listed the desire to protect national industrial interests, fickle political leadership, and lack of trust in handling sensitive information as key problems needing to be overcome.[43] This thesis could benefit from incorporating the direct, practical examples of European efforts at coalition space operations when considering how the United States might work in a similar capacity with France.

Thus, this work seeks to answer, in a novel way, the thesis question, "How might the United States benefit from coalition operations in space?" In its approach, it gives more emphasis to overcoming "cultural differences" than has existing literature on coalition operations in space. Furthermore, this work seeks to inform the larger methodological debate about collective approaches to space security, which is linked to the United States' current space security strategy, focused on deterrence. It does this by expanding the scope of this methodological debate to consider how to further engage partner nations in coalition operations in space.

D.   RESEARCH DESIGN

The research to support this thesis consists of comparative case studies of France, Australia, and Japan, delving into the politics of each country's relations with the United States, a brief history of the country's cooperation in space with the United States, and a qualitative assessment of the country's military space capabilities. It pulls this information from a variety of written French and English language sources.

E.   THESIS OVERVIEW AND CHAPTER OUTLINE

Following the introductory chapter, this thesis devotes one chapter each to France, Australia, and Japan. The final chapter consists of comparative analysis and policy recommendations. The chapters on each of the three countries have four parts, identified alphabetically: part A, a discussion of the military space politics of the country and its

---

[43] Heisbourg and Pasco, *Espace Militaire*, 128–129.

disposition to collaborate with the United States; part B, a brief history of the space cooperation between the country and the United States; part C, a presentation of the military space capabilities that the country possesses; and part D, analysis and recommendations based on the preceding parts.

II.   FRANCE

This chapter on French military space activities has four parts. The first part describes the strategic direction of France's military space efforts and touches upon French predisposition to collaborate with the United States in this domain. The second part briefly describes the historical collaboration and mutual influence that the French and American space efforts have had on one another. The third part describes the organization and capabilities of France's military space effort. The last part analyzes the preceding three parts to present the areas in which United States Department of Defense might benefit from closer military space collaboration with the French Defense Ministry.

A.   STRATEGIC DIRECTION AND PREDISPOSITION TO COLLABORATE

Part A presents a series of developments that have affected French military space activities from the founding of the North Atlantic Treaty Alliance to the present. These developments include France's nuclear program; its participation in the European Launcher Development Organization (ELDO) and the European Space Agency (ESA); French advances in SATCOM, remote sensing from space, and space launch; and the increased focus that the French government has placed on military space activities since 2008. These developments warrant our attention since they are closely related to the barriers to security cooperation in space presented in chapter 1:   lack of firm political leadership, realistic milestones, adequate technological capabilities, and trust in handling sensitive information.

France has been a formal ally of the United States since signing the North Atlantic Treaty in 1949. A key consideration at the time was how France and the United States should respond to the growing threat posed by the Soviet Union to North America and especially to Europe. The North Atlantic Treaty prescribed the development of a unified military command structure to deal with the Soviet threat and recognized that an attack of one alliance member in Europe or North America would be responded to as an attack against them all.[44]

The first successful explosion of an atomic bomb by France in 1960 would fundamentally shape France's military space program and its security relationship with the United States for the next half century. In the 1960s and into the early 1970s, for example, France would invest funds into its nuclear efforts that could have gone into developing military satellite capabilities. For its part, the United States would take steps to prevent France from acquiring a missile delivery system for its nuclear weapons. When the French finally overcame American preventative measures to develop an independent launch capability, albeit by developing a rocket for a civilian space program, it would have profound effects on the commercial space launch market and the viability of ESA, starting in the 1970s.

From 1958 until 1969, Charles de Gaulle would serve as the president of France. In addition to his desire for an independent nuclear capability, President de Gaulle's dislike for supra-national organizations and the role that he envisioned for France in Europe would shape the country's space activities during those formative years. In 1966, France withdrew from NATO's command structure. Tellingly, perhaps, France would rejoin the NATO command in 2009, during the period in which its interests in space also began to re-align with the security interests of the United States. In addition to NATO, de Gaulle did not look very favorably upon the European Economic Community either. Thus, when France began to search for an economical way to develop a satellite launch capability, its political requirements would shape the approach it took.

In the same year that it left NATO, France established a space port, the Guiana Space Center (Centre Spatial Guyanais) at Kourou (French Guiana).[45] What it lacked until 1979, however, was a satellite launch vehicle. In 1962, France was one of seven European

---

[44] Australia Broadcasting Corporation, "Fact check: Does ANZUS Commit the U.S. to Come to Australia's Aid?," *ABC News*, July 22, 2014, http://www.abc.net.au/news/2014-07-08/does-anzus-commit-us-to-come-to-australias-aid-fact-check/5559288.

[45] Sébastien Matte la Faveur, "The Interest and Opposition of the French Military in Satellite Reconnaissance for France: A Talk with a General Officer of the French Forces," *Space Chronicle*, vol. 59, sup. 1, 2006, 1–9.

countries to sign the Convention of the European Launcher Development Organization, created without sponsorship from the Organization for European Economic Cooperation, which would have permitted U.S. participation in ELDO.[46] In the coming years, ELDO would flounder under political demands placed on it, in part, by France.

In the 1970s, France was in a better position to participate in the creation of a new European space organization following de Gaulle's resignation and replacement. In 1975, France participated in the establishment of ESA.[47] French-led development of the Ariane rocket, first launched in 1979, proved crucial to ESA's success.[48] The commercial arm for the Ariane program, Arianespace, would capture about 50 percent of the commercial launch market by 1985.[49]

Long focused on its independent strategic nuclear program and associated air- and sea-based delivery systems, France was able to devote more funds to its non-nuclear systems in the 1970s. The French government mandated the development of military reconnaissance and communications satellites for the first time in the 1977–1982 defense budget (Loi de Programmation Militaire [LPM]).[50] This resulted in the *Syracuse* (*Systeme de Radio Communications Utilisant un Satellite*) communications satellite program, which began in 1980. The first dual-use Syracuse satellite, *Télécom 1A*, was launched on an Ariane rocket in 1984.[51] For imagery, the defense ministry would agree to help fund France's civil space program, CNES (Centre National d'Etudes Spatiales), to develop the first *SPOT* (*Système Probatoire d'Observation de la Terre*) satellite. The availability of *SPOT* satellite images on the commercial market would increase the commercial orientation of the U.S. military space reconnaissance program, as examined in part B.

---

[46] Michael Sheehan, "Chapter 5: European Integration and Space," *The International Politics of Space* (New York: Routledge 2007), 77–78.

[47] Sheehan, "European Integration and Space," 82–83.

[48] Sheehan, "European Integration and Space," 85.

[49] John Krige, Angelina Long Cahhahan, and Ashok Mahara, *NASA in the World: Fifty Years of International Collaboration in Space* (New York: Palgrave Macmillan, 2013), 4.

[50] Matte la Faveur, "The Interest and the Opposition," 3.

[51] Gunter Dirk Krebs, "Télécom 1A, 1B, 1C," *Gunter's Space Page*, http://space.skyrocket.de/doc_sdat/telecom-1.htm (accessed March 11, 2018).

France then launched its first proper military reconnaissance satellite, *Helios 1A*, in 1995. It would embark upon the creation of a second generation of military reconnaissance and communications satellites in the 1990s and early 2000s.

French products also began to provide an alternative to American commercial satellite technology starting in the late 1990s. Notably, when the export and use of U.S. manufactured space technology was restricted by aggressive U.S. International Trafficking in Arms Regulations (ITAR) from 1998 and until roughly 2013, the French aerospace firm Alcatel-Alenia spearheaded an effort to market and sell "ITAR-free" products.[52] Several of the ways in which U.S. policy contributed to the development of the French ability to rival U.S. products in space is, once again, presented in part B.

Following a falling out between France and the United States during the early 2000s over events leading up to the U.S. led invasion of Iraq, a rapprochement of French and American security-interests began to occur during the Sarkozy presidency (2007-2012). In 2008, the Sarkozy administration addressed the subject of space security significantly in a white paper on security and defense (Défense et Sécurité nationale: le Livre blanc). Serving as a defense review, the white paper elevated space's importance on the French national security agenda, much as the Space Commission's report had done for military space in the United States in 2001. Several key points from the 2008 white paper pertaining to the French use of outer space were: recognition that the employment of all nature of satellites —communication, observation, signals, warning, navigation, weather, etc.—had become indispensable to French military-strategic functions; opposition to a war in space; a proclivity to avoid weaponizing space; the need to align investments in space capabilities with strategic defense needs; and the placement of space doctrine, operations, and programs under a Joint Space Command (Commandement interarmées de l'espace [CIE]) commandant responsible directly to the French Armed Forces Chief of Staff.[53] These

---

[52] Amy Svitak, "U.S. Electronics Firm Fined $8 million for Export Violations: As U.S. Loosens Satellite Export Rules, Suppliers Own Up to Violations," *Aviation Week*, September 16, 2013, http://aviationweek.com/awin/us-electronics-firm-fined-8-million-export-violations.

[53] Jean-Claude Mallet, *Défense et Sécurité Nationale: le Livre Blanc*, June 2008, 143, http://www. ladocumentation francaise.fr/var/storage/rapports-publics/084000341.pdf [translated by the author].

policy changes would lead to more direct military collaboration in space, and a more stable foundation on which such collaboration could occur, as shown in the following paragraphs.

Despite financial setbacks after 2008, France made concerted efforts to realize its vision of space security following the release of the white paper. A formal draft of the Code of Conduct for Outer Space Activities appeared before the European Union (EU) during the French presidency of that institution.[54] The draft code later made its way into official consultations among members of the United Nations (UN) in 2013 and 2014. The United States supported the draft code by the 2013 consultations, only for the European-led initiative to die over procedural issues raised by Russia and China two years later.[55]

Similarly, the French military established the billet of the CIE commandant in 2010. In 2016, the CIE commandant reported to the French National Assembly on his command and on France's ongoing military space efforts for the first time. His testimony was followed by testimony of the current commandant in December 2017. The most recent testimony was particularly well attended by members of the National Assembly, reflecting the current level of French interest in national-security space issues.[56]

The CIE has seemingly helped the French military to realize its military space agenda by giving a more pragmatic focus to France's military space program. This naturally benefits the United States, addressing the need to develop realistic milestones. Prior to the creation of the CIE, France's military space community was working to meet many different operator and user requirements with its available assets.[57] Since its creation, the CIE has helped to set a unified agenda by overseeing the work of four offices

---

54 Chris Johnson, "Draft International Code of Conduct for Outer Space Activities Fact Sheet," *Secure World Foundation*, February 2015, https://swfound.org/media/166384/swf_draft_international_code_of_ conduct_for_outer_space_activities_fact_sheet_february_2014.pdf.

55 Gabriella Irsten, "The Consultation Process for the International Code of Conduct for Outer Space Activities Ends," *Reaching Critical Will*, accessed February 25, 2018, http://reachingcriticalwill.org/news/ latest-news/8907-the-consultation-process-for-the-international-code-of-conduct-for-outer-space-activities-ends.

56 *French National Assembly, Commission of the Armed Forces and National Defense*, 25th leg., (December 20, 2017) (statement of Jean-Jacques Bridey, president of the commission), 7 [translated by the author]. The president of the commission notes that "very numerous colleagues" had questions. This comment and the number of people present indicate a high level of interest.

57 *French National Assembly, Commission of the Armed Forces and National Defense*, 24th leg., (May 17, 2016,) (testimony of Jean-Daniel Testé, Joint Space Commandant), 4 [translated by the author].

responsible for military space functions at the operational level and the work of military officers employed at the technical level. The CIE is charged with identifying the needs of the French Army, Navy, and Air Force, managing the use of space assets to coordinate their employment in meeting those needs, and participating in the planning and realization of space efforts with international partners. Consequently, it has become the entry point in France for all questions related to the military space competencies.

Despite an announcement in 2008 that France would double its spending on military space applications to 800 million euros annually, the reality of France's financial situation following the 2008 financial crisis has prevented it from fully realizing that goal through 2017.[58] Thus, France devoted only 335 million euros to its military space program in 2013, when the Hollande administration conducted a defense review oriented at maintaining the status quo of France's defense in a period of fiscal austerity.[59][60] This sum was increased to 596 million euros by 2015, however, probably linked to the French military's requirement to replace eight satellites between 2018 and 2021.[61]

At the direction of President Macron, the French defense minister presented the findings of its 2017 strategic defense review last October. The intent of this latest review was to frame the strategic security environment for France's 2019–2025 LPM.[62] This framing was meant to facilitate the French government's efforts to prioritize its investments in defense, including in space defense, in the coming years. France's military space activities fare well in this review.

---

[58] Heisbourg and Pasco, *Espace Militaire*, 8.

[59] Nathalie Guibert, "French White Paper Tries to Reconcile Strategic Ambitions/Budget," *Fortuna's Corner*, April 29, 2013, https://fortunascorner.com/2013/04/30/french-white-paper-tries-to-reconcile-strategic-ambitionsbudget/.

[60] *French National Assembly*, Testé, 8.

[61] *French National Assembly, Commission of the Armed Forces and National Defense*, 25th leg., (December 20, 2017) (testimony of Jean-Pascal Breton, Joint Space Commandant), 3.

[62] Direction Générale des Relations Internationales et de la Stratégie, "Revue Stratégique : Une Analyse Lucide et Volontariste pour Préparer la Prochaine Loi de Programmation Militaire," April 12, 2017, https:// www.defense.gouv.fr/dgris/presentation/evenements/revue-strategique-de-defense-et-de-securite-nationale-2017 [translated by the author].

In its findings, the defense ministry describes the space environment as being in a period of profound change.[63] Changes to the space environment have been characterized by military and strategic competition as well as by a large increase in the number of state and private actors with easy access to space according to the review; this evolution and the unprecedented technological evolution that underpins it are pointing toward a new way of thinking about and exploiting space systems. The review notes that this new way of thinking and acting has brought with it an increased risk of confrontation in space, as countries may be tempted, now more than ever before, to deny their rivals access to space or to disrupt the operations of their space systems; furthermore, countries now have the opportunity to openly fund anti-satellite technologies, such as advances in electric-propulsion and robotics, under the guise of civil programs, since so many space technologies are dual-use now. The defense ministry notes, similarly, that it is concerned that countries may employ a variety of non-kinetic means to damage a rival's space assets without running the risk of detection associated with a traditional kinetic attack.

Faced with a growing number of threats to its space systems, the French military is still attempting to rise to the challenge on a still rather modest budget relative to France's own civil space budget and relative to the U.S. military space budget, of course. Even with recent increases, France's military space budget amounts to only one-fourth of the budget provided to CNES.[64] By point of comparison, the U.S. military space budget reached parity with NASA's budget around 1981 and now greatly exceeds it. NASA's budget significantly exceeded the current French budget even in 1981.[65]

Part of the French military's response to its financial and technical challenges to date has been to seek increased international partnering. For example, it will use funding acquired from the European Union Space Surveillance and Tracking program to renovate

---

[63] Ministère des Armées, *Revue Stratégique de Défense et De Sécurité Nationale*, October 13, 2017, 45–46, https://www.defense.gouv.fr/dgris/politique-de-defense/revue-strategique/revue-strategique [translated by the author].

[64] Testé projects an expenditure of 596 million Euros and 542 million Euros for 2015 and 2019 respectively; see *French National Assembly*, Testé, 8. CNES reported a budget of 2334 million Euros for 2017; see CNES, "Le 2eme Budget au Monde," January 6, 2017, https://cnes.fr/fr/web/CNES-fr/11507-le-2eme-budget-au-monde.php.

[65] Krige, et al., *NASA in the World*, 4.

its GRAVES (Grand Réseau Adapté à la Veille Spatiale) satellite surveillance radar.[66] The French military is also exploring opportunities for closer cooperative projects with its traditional strategic partners, particularly Germany, as well as closer cooperation with the U.S. Department of Defense in certain areas. In this regard, the current CIE commandant stated in his testimony before the National Assembly that the United States had provided the French military with access to its classified space catalog, normally available only to the Five-Eye countries.[67] In addition to increased partnering, the French military is requesting funds to modernize its capabilities for monitoring objects in low-Earth-orbit, funds to upgrade the information systems it uses for space-security, and funds to sponsor studies related to monitoring the geostationary satellite belt in the next LPM.[68] Fortunately, with France's overall defense spending set to grow to two percent of the gross domestic product by 2025, the military space budget appears likely to increase as well.[69]

B.   HISTORICAL COLLABORATION

Part B briefly describes how historical interaction between French and American military, civil, and commercial space entities has contributed to the development of France as a space power today, especially in the areas of space launch and Earth imagining. It also shows some of the second- and third- order effects of previous U.S. policies on technology sharing, international collaboration, and business that continue to resonate. This information is pertinent when the potential for wider collaboration is considered, extending beyond the narrow confines of jointly manning a satellite watch floor to broader decisions such as whether to adopt policies more or less favorable to an ally's commercial space industry, for instance.

The U.S. Space Act of 1958 mandated an organization to pursue both international collaboration and space leadership and brought the National Aeronautics and Space

---

[66] *French National Assembly*, Breton, 6.

[67] *French National Assembly*, Breton, 6.

[68] *French National Assembly*, Breton, 5.

[69] Agence France Presse, "Philippe Annonce une Hausse sans Précédent du Budget de la Défense," *Le Figaro*, August 9, 2017, http://www.lefigaro.fr/conjoncture/2017/09/08/20002-20170908ARTFIG00082-philippe-annonce-une-hausse-sans-precedent-du-budget-de-la-defense.php [translated by the author].

Administration (NASA) into existence.[70] NASA's second director of the Office of International Programs, Arnold W. Frutkin, significantly influenced the institution's approach to international collaboration during his tenure, lasting from 1959 to 1979.[71] The criteria that he set for international collaboration meant that NASA would favor projects with countries that possessed significant wealth and industrial capacity. Upon coming to power in 1958, President de Gaulle was determined to strengthen France's technological and industrial capacity, which logically contributed to NASA favoring projects with France.[72]

Early in de Gaulle's tenure, the French pursued improvements to the Veronique (Vernon Electronique) sounding rocket, three of which they launched from Algeria in March 1959.[73] The Veronique rockets complemented the development of France's nuclear force de frappe (strike force). Moreover, the sodium mixture that the Veronique delivered into the upper atmosphere helped scientists to improve their understanding of atmospheric winds and turbulences. Prior to the rocket's first launch, a French scientist Jacques Blamont had brought a key piece of hardware used to expel this sodium mixture from the Veronique rockets home to France with him from the Air Force Cambridge Research Laboratories, located near Boston.[74]

Success with the Veronique rockets reinforced French public interest in a national space program. The French national space agency CNES was born in 1961 with the attendant expenses that it incurred. That same year, NASA agreed to launch worthy French experiments and scientific payloads and to host French scientists in NASA centers.[75][76] This agreement stemmed from an initiative that the American delegate to the Committee

---

[70] Krige et al., *NASA in the World*, 4.

[71] Krige et al., *NASA in the World*, 7–13.

[72] Krige et al., *NASA in the World*, 28.

[73] CNES, "Les 50 Ans de Veronique," March 26, 2009, https://cnes.fr/en/web/CNES-fr/7527-les-50-ans-de-veronique.php [translated by the author].

[74] Krige et al., *NASA in the World*, 28.

[75] Krige et al., *NASA in the World*, 29.

[76] John Krige, in *Science and Technology in the Global Cold War*, ed. Naomi Oreskes (Cambridge, Mass.: The MIT Press, 2014), 230.

on Space Research (COSPAR) had proposed in 1959. The COSPAR initiative and the agreement made in 1961 led to the development of the *FR-1* satellite, jointly sponsored by NASA and CNES.[77] NASA used a Scout rocket to launch the *FR-1* satellite into orbit in 1965, making it the first French scientific satellite and the first satellite developed by CNES.[78][79]

Collaboration during the *FR-1* project led to the development of commercial ties between high technology firms in France and the United States.[80] As an example, the French firm Mécanique Aviation Traction and the American firm Thompson Ramo Wooldridge (TRW) developed an especially close relationship. As a result, Mécanique Aviation Traction gained access to TRW patents and know-how through a "Technical Assistance and Licensing Agreement," while TRW bolstered its international image in an effort to win a contract with Communications Satellite Corporation (Comsat). This interaction logically contributed to the development of France's nascent space industry.

NASA launched Comsat's *Early Bird* satellite to a geostationary orbit in 1965.[81] For its part, Comsat contracted TRW to build its third generation of International Telecommunications Satellites Organization (Intelsat) satellites.[82] Comsat enabled speedy global coverage, effective competition, foreign participation, and nondiscriminatory system access, although its commercial orientation would pose certain challenges to governmental space collaboration in the coming years.

---

[77] Krige et al., *NASA in the World*, 29.

[78] NASA, "FR1," March 21, 2017, https://nssdc.gsfc.nasa.gov/nmc/spacecraftDisplay.do?id=1965-101A.

[79] CNES, "FR-1, le 1er satellite du CNES en 1965," January 22, 2015, https://www.youtube.com/watch?v=NIS_cDyc9PI [translated by the author].

[80] Krige et al., *NASA in the World*, 29.

[81] CNES, "Le Programme *Symphonie*," accessed February 16, 2018, http://www.cnes-observatoire.net/actualites/actu2/73_appel-a-projet-symphonie/Symphonie_Synthese_fr.pdf [translated by the author].

[82] "COMSAT Corporation," Company-Histories.com, 1998, accessed March 9, 2018, http://www.company-histories.com/COMSAT-Corporation-Company-History.html

Unfortunately, *Early Bird's* success served to unite French and German concerns over an American monopoly on satellite television and radio programming.[83] In part, this was due to the cultural programming that television and radio programming implied. French and German concern with American influence resulted in the creation of a Franco-German satellite telecommunications group in 1966. The group started the joint telecommunications satellite program *Symphonie* that same year. The *Symphonie* satellite program offered a political windfall for French and German politicians hoping for closer relations between the two countries. Moreover, the program was able to produce two flight-ready *Symphonie* satellites in 1974 and 1975.

As the first *Symphonie* satellite neared completion, the French and their German counterparts were challenged by how to launch it. Signed in 1964, National Security Action Memorandum 294 precluded American contribution or assistance to the development of a delivery system for France's national strategic nuclear capability.[84] Therefore, the United States would not have assisted France in the development of a heavy lift rocket to launch the satellite. Furthermore, in signing National Security Action Memorandum 338 the following year, President Johnson concurred with the recommendation of one of his advisors that the United States "should not consider requests for launch services or other assistance in the development of communications for commercial purposes" except as benefitted the single global commercial SATCOM network the U.S. government was trying to establish, i.e., the Comsat network.[85] Lest the Nixon administration should change its policy, Comsat Chief Executive Officer Joseph Charyk continued to drive home his company's opposition to the U.S. assisting other countries in launching their commercial communication satellites in communications with the State Department through at least 1970.[86]

---

[83] CNES, "Le Programme Symphonie."

[84] Krige et al., *NASA in the World,* 53–54.

[85] James O'Connell, "Memorandum concerning U.S assistance in the development of foreign communications satellite capabilities," September 17, 1965, in *Exploring the Unknown: Select Documents in the History of the U.S. Civilian Space Program*, vol. 3, ed. John M. Logsdon (Washington,DC: NASA, 1998), 93.

[86] Krige et al., *NASA in the World,* 90.

France's participation in ELDO was intended to provide it with a capability to launch a communication satellite into a geostationary orbit. In 1966, ELDO committed to developing the Europa II rocket, which would have been capable of lifting a 200-kilogram satellite to geostationary orbit in the event of the rocket's successful development and production.[87] However, Great Britain's announcement in 1968 that it would withdraw financial support to ELDO in 1971 would ultimately doom the launcher. France committed itself to producing the Ariane launcher in late 1972 as a result. Unfortunately, this left the Europeans without a European launcher for the *Symphonie* satellites.

As a result of these developments, the directors of Franco-German satellite project had turned to NASA as early as 1968 to request Atlas or Thor Delta rockets to launch the *Symphonie* satellites.[88] NASA agreed to their requests to furnish the rockets provided that an agreement could be reached on the experimental character of the *Symphonie* project. After negotiations lasting through 1974, NASA's requirement that the satellites be experimental in character resulted in France and Germany having to renounce commercial exploitation of the *Symphonie* satellites for most of their design life. NASA thus agreed to launch the satellites. Nevertheless, the loss of revenue and the associated embarrassment caused by NASA's reluctance to launch the *Symphonie* satellites fueled calls for an independent European launch capability, which the Ariane rocket later provided. In an effort to project this capacity, France very recently supported a proposal to launch all state-owned European satellites on European launchers.[89]

Turning to the subject of collaboration in Earth imaging, NASA stirred public interest in aerial photography from the earliest manned space flights. Project Mercury astronauts took photographs specifically for geological purposes in 1962 and 1963.[90] The

---

[87] Sheehan, "European Integration and Space," 80–81.

[88] Lorenza Sebesta, "Chapter 11, U.S.-European Relations and the Decision to Build Ariane, the European Launch Vehicle," *SP-4217 Beyond the Ionosphere*, ed. Andrew Butrica, January 21, 2013, https://history.nasa. gov/SP-4217/ch11.htm.

[89] *French National Assembly*, Breton, 12.

[90] Paul D. Lowman Jr., "Geologic Orbital Photography: Experience from the Gemini Program," June 1968, 1, https://ntrs.nasa.gov/archive/nasa/casi.ntrs.nasa.gov/19680018143.pdf.

Synoptic Terrain Photography Experiment during the Gemini program produced nearly 1,100 geologically useful photographs in 1965 and 1966.

NASA's experiments at collecting and analyzing Earth imagery inspired the Director of the U.S. Geological Survey. He put forth the idea of collecting information about the planet's natural resources from a remote-sensing satellite in 1965.[91] Despite objections to the program raised by the Department of Defense, which was worried about the implications for its then-secret Keyhole satellite programs, the U.S. Secretary of the Interior announced the establishment of the Earth Resources Observation Satellite Program in 1966.[92] NASA received approval to build the first satellite in 1970 as part of the Earth Resources Observation Satellite Program.[93] In July 1972, NASA launched *Earth Resources Technology Satellite*, later named *Landsat-1*.

NASA actively distributed Landsat data and taught people how to use it. Motivated in part by the Earth Resources Observation Satellite Program, as well as by military and commercial interests, France embarked upon the military satellite observation program (*Satellite Militaire d'Observation Optique*), which it later cancelled, and the civilian *SPOT* satellite program in 1977 and 1978, respectively.[94]

In 1982, the French Ministry of Defense created an image interpretation center within its armament directorate to analyze Landsat images and to train military photo-analysts in preparation for the *SPOT* satellites. In 1986, CNES launched the first *SPOT* satellite. The French army established a reconnaissance section (Section d'Etude de Documentation et d'Images) to exploit *SPOT* images that same year.

In 1990, the U.S. Army signed an agreement to receive *SPOT* images.[95] Following operation Desert Storm, the U.S. Air Force also purchased the Eagle Vision system to

---

[91] Paul R. Baumann, "History of Remote Sensing, Satellite Imagery, Part II," Suny Oneonta College, 2009, https://www.oneonta.edu/faculty/baumanpr/geosat2/RS%20History%20II/RS-History-Part-2.html.

[92] United States Geological Survey," Earth Resources Observation Satellite (EROS) Program," 1, https://eros.usgs.gov/sites/all/files/external/eros/history/1970s/Documents/1966-1977_Earth_Resources_Observation_Systems %28EROS%29_Program.pdf.

[93] Baumann, "History of Remote Sensing, Satellite Imagery, Part II."

[94] Matte la Faveur, "The Interest and Opposition," 3–8.

[95] Matte la Faveur, "The Interest and Opposition," 8.

receive and process downlinked *SPOT* images.[96] Thanks to the capability and commercial success of the *SPOT* satellites, France took the lead in the world market for satellite imagery in the 1990s.[97] The U.S. military makes wide use of commercial Earth imaging satellites today.

C.   CURRENT MILITARY SPACE ORGANIZATION AND CAPABILITIES

Part C describes the organization and capabilities of France's military space program. This description starts with CIE's organization. It then turns to France's increasing military space capability and associated external service providers. Part C is directly relevant to topics such as the CSpO initiative, providing the who and what for current military-to-military collaboration with France in space.

As discussed in part A, the billet for the CIE commandant was created in 2010. A member of the Joint Command in Paris, the CIE commandant reports to the operations chief on the Joint Chiefs of Staff while serving under the direct authority of the chairman of the Joint Chiefs of Staff.[98][99] An Air Force brigadier general has filled the CIE commandant billet since its creation. As a point of comparison with the U.S. military hierarchy, the U.S. Air Force sent a brigadier general, the U.S. Strategic Command deputy director of global operations, to sign an advanced Space Situational Awareness (SSA) agreement with the CIE commandant in 2015.[100] The Department of State sent the deputy assistant secretary for space policy.

At the operational-level, the CIE subsumed four offices related to space defense under a single military commander upon its creation. The offices falling under the CIE currently are the Office of Space Policy and Cooperation (Bureau Politique Spatiale et

---

[96] Roger George and Robert Kline, *Intelligence and the National Security Strategist: Enduring Issues and Challenges* (Lanham, Md.: Rowman & Littlefield, 2006), 155.

[97] Claverie et al., "Towards disruptions," 417.

[98] Ministère des Armées, "Le Commandement Interarmées de l'Espace," March 26, 2012, https://www.defense.gouv .fr/actualites/dossiers/l-espace-au-profit-des-operations-militaires/fiches-techniques/cie [translated by the author].

[99] *French National Assembly*, Breton, 2.

[100] Mike Gruss, "U.S., France Expand Data-sharing Agreement," *SpaceNews*, April 16, 2015, http://spacenews.com/us-france-expand-space-data-sharing-agreement/.

Coopérations), the Office of Future Planning (Bureau Préparation de l'Avenir), the Office of Coordination and Employment (Bureau Emploi et Coordination), and the Office of Exploitation of the Space Environment (Bureau Maîtrise de l'Environnement Spatial).[101] As the name suggests, the Office of Space Policy and Cooperation coordinates joint space policy and international and multilateral cooperation. The Office of Future Planning determines operational needs and leads the acquisitions of space systems. The Office of Coordination and Employment manages and directs the employment of military space assets. The Office of Exploitation of the Space Environment is charged with managing space situational awareness and space control, gathering intelligence of the international situation in space, and the development of space subject matter expertise in the French armed forces.

The work of these four offices structures and organizes work at the technical space-operations level. Technical operations are organized into six competencies: observation, signals, space surveillance, missile warning, telecommunications, and position, navigation, and timing (PNT). Officers working at the technical level gather the military's requirements and participate in the acquisition of products that optimize the utilization of existing space-assets. Currently, France's military services do not have a dedicated cadre of space professionals; however, the CIE is in the process of determining the competencies and training required to put one in place.[102]

As the French military's subject-matter expert on space, the CIE advises the civil authorities and different bodies within the defense ministry. These bodies include the Air Defense and Air Operations Command (Commandement de la Défense Aérienne et des Opérations Aériennes), the Joint Directorate of Network Infrastructure and Defense Information Systems (Direction Interarmées des Réseaux d'Infrastructure et des Systèmes d'Information de la Défense), and the Military Intelligence Directorate (Direction du Renseignement Militaire).[103]

---

101 *French National Assembly*, Testé, 5.

102 *French National Assembly*, Breton, 16–17.

103 *French National Assembly*, Breton, 2.

The CIE has at its disposition satellites covering the areas of Earth observation, signals intelligence, satellite communications, PNT systems, and space surveillance.[104] This section now turns to discussing the French military's capabilities in the above mission areas, as well as briefly touching upon the environmental monitoring and space launch capabilities to which it also maintains access. It proceeds from discussing electro-optical capabilities to discussing those associated with signals intelligence, satellite communications, PNT systems, space situational awareness, and finally space launch.

In 2016, the CIE acquired 45,883 satellite images, approximately 10 percent more than the year prior.[105] This is an average of 125 images per day taken around the globe. The need for satellite imagery is growing, especially in view of France's current level of military engagement.

In the area of Earth observation, the military currently employs two *Helios-II* satellites, launched in 2004 and 2009, and two *Pléiades* satellites, launched in 2011 and 2012. All of the satellites maintain sun-synchronous orbits. The *Helios-II* satellites provide imagery estimated at .35 m resolution from 700 km altitude. The *Pléiades* satellites provide .50 m resolution panchromatic imagery and 2 m resolution multi-spectral imagery from approximately the same altitude as the *Helios-II* satellites.[106][107] *Pléiades* is a dual-use, commercial and military, satellite that permits daytime visible and nighttime infrared imaging.[108] Operating in pairs, the *Pléiades* satellites can be used for change detection analysis. The French military also has access to radar imagery thanks to exchange agreements with the Germans and the Italians. These agreements provides it with access to imagery from the *SAR-Lupe* (*Synthetic Aperture Radar-Lupe*) and *COSMO-SkyMed*

---

104 *French National Assembly*, Breton, 3.

105 *French National Assembly*, Breton, 3.

106 Peter B. de Selding, "French Helios 2B Spy Sat Sends Back First Test Images," *SpaceNews*, January 4, 2010, http://spacenews.com/32557french-helios-2b-spy-sat-sends-back-first-test-images/.

107 Harris Geospatial Solutions, "Pléiades: from Airbus Defense and Space," accessed February 19, 2018, http://www.harrisgeospatial.com/DataImagery/SatelliteImagery/HighResolution/Pleiades.aspx.

108 *French National Assembly*, Breton, 6.

(*Constellation of Small Satellites for the Mediterranean Basin Observation-SkyMed*) radar satellites.[109]

In 2016, the CIE commandant estimated that the French military would gain access to 650 images per day when all three of France's new *CSO* (*Composante Spatiale Optique*) satellites were operational in 2021.[110] The satellites will operate in polar orbits at 800 km or at 480 km altitude depending on the mission of the individual satellite. These images will be at a higher quality and across a greater number of spectral bands compared to the French military's current satellite capabilities.[111] The *CSO* satellites are expected to last for 10 years, with the first *CSO* satellite being launched at the end of this year.[112] CNES will oversee satellite maintenance and ground-station operations, presumably from its technical and operational complex in Toulouse, France.[113][114]

France has restructured the stillborn *MUSIS* (*Multinational Space-based Imaging System*) satellite program through its development of the *CSO* satellites.[115] Whereas the use of the *Helios-II* satellites is scheduled among partner nations, and *MUSIS* was planned to pursue this type of scheduling, the French will control the scheduling of the *CSO* satellites once they are on-orbit. Germany and Sweden, France's current partners in the *CSO* satellite program, will be granted access to a certain percentage of the satellites' images based on their respective contributions to the program.

In 2008, all five countries participating in the *Helios-II* program, led by France, agreed to provide *Helios-II* imagery to the EU Satellite Centre.[116] Directed by a French

---

[109] *French National Assembly*, Testé, 5.

[110] CNES, "CSO/MUSIS," May 30, 2015, https://cso.cnes.fr/en/csomusis-0.

[111] *French National Assembly*, Testé, 6.

[112] CNES, "CSO/MUSIS."

[113] CNES, "CSO/MUSIS."

[114] CNES, "CNES Facilities," February 18, 2003, https://cnes.fr/en/web/CNES-en/3801-cnes-facilities.php.

[115] *French National Assembly*, Breton, 4.

[116] France Diplomatie, "France's Role in European Space Policy," accessed March 4, 2018, https://www.diplomatie.gouv.fr/en/french-foreign-policy/scientific-diplomacy/cooperation-in-the-space-sector/article/france-s-role-in-european-space.

general since 2015, the Satellite Centre supports the EU's Common Foreign and Security Policy and its Common Security and Defense Policy in particular.[117][118] In 2016, the Satellite Centre delivered 1,846 geospatial and imagery intelligence products to various EU civil and military entities and projects.[119] The Satellite Centre sourced most of the images used in these products from commercial providers.[120]

France has developed not only the satellites but also the means of exploiting the information gathered by its signals intelligence satellites in recent years.[121] The four *ELISA* (*Electronic Intelligence Satellite*) satellites are part of a French experimental satellite program aimed at mastering the technology required for electronic intelligence collection. Like France's other intelligence, surveillance, and reconnaissance satellites, the *ELISA* satellites are employed in a sun-synchronous orbit. This group of satellites will stay in service until the middle of 2020, with the *CERES* (*Capacité de Renseignement Électromagnétique Spatiale*) satellites replacing the *ELISA* satellites before the end of that year. The *CERES* satellites will be the French military's first dedicated ELINT satellites. CNES will operate and track these satellites.[122]

Of note, given its role in operating military satellites, CNES is a state-controlled entity of an industrial or commercial nature (Etablissement Public à Caractère Industriel et Commercial)[123] CNES provides its expertise in the space domain to the French military through the Joint Chiefs of Staff, principally in coordination with the armament directorate,

---

117 EU Satellite Centre, *EU Satellite Centre Annual Report 2015*, 2016, 7, https://www.satcen.europa. eu/key_documents/EU%20SatCen%20Annual%20Report%202015571e3f8bf9d72519a0411205.pdf.

118 *French National Assembly*, Breton, 18.

119 EU Satellite Centre, *EU Satellite Centre Annual Report 2016,* 2017, 13–16, https://www.satcen. europa.eu/key_documents/EU%20SatCen%20Annual%20Report%20201658e24cb1f9d7202538bed52b. pdf.

120 EU Satellite, EU Satellite Centre Annual Report 2016, 10.

121 *French National Assembly*, Breton, 4.

122 CNES, "CERES," June 10, 2015, https://ceres.cnes.fr/en/ceres-2.

123 CNES, "La France Célèbre les 50 Ans de son Agence Spatiale," 2011, https://cnes.fr/sites/default/ files/ migration/automne/standard/2014_10/p9701_0c600498df91d62c08ba06c5143f7e0aDP_50_ans_ CNES.pdf, 2 [translated by the author].

and it receives a portion of its funding from the military.[124][125] CNES engages under private contract around 2,400 employees, mostly engineers. These employees are divided among centers in four locations: Evry (launch directorate), Korou (launch base), Paris (headquarters), and Toulouse (orbital systems). Around 70 percent of CNES employees are located at the Toulouse center.[126]

The French military employs four geostationary telecommunications satellites: two *Syracuse-3* (*Systeme de Radio Communications Utilisant un Satellite-3*), plus two total *Sicral-2* (*Sistema Italiana de Communicazione Riservente Allarmi-2*) and *Athena-Fidus* (*Access on Theatres and European Nations for Allied Forces - French Italian Dual Use Satellite*) satellites, whose capacity is shared with Italy.[127] One Syracuse satellite is located over West Africa; the other three satellites are located over the Middle East.[128] The Syracuse-3 satellites are nuclear hardened and resistant to jamming, permit interoperability according to NATO standards, and allow for SHF and EHF communications.[129][130] Italy is the majority owner of the UHF/SHF *Sicral-2* satellite; France is allocated frequency in the SHF range only on this satellite.[131] The *Sicral-2* satellite meets NATO compatibility standards like the first two *Syracuse-3* satellites and the third, planned *Syracuse-3* satellite, which it effectively replaced. With the *Athena-Fidus* satellite, France operates five of the

124 CNES, "La France célèbre," 3.

125 *French National Assembly*, Breton, 15.

126 CNES, "La France célèbre," 2.

127 *French National Assembly*, Testé, 5.

128 "Geostationary Satellites," *N2YO.com - Real Time Satellite Tracking and Predictions*, accessed February 28, 2018, https://n2yo.com/satellites /?c=10.

129 Thales Group, "Syracuse II: Satellite Communications Leveraging Joint C4ISR Capabilities," accessed February 19, 2018, https://www. thalesgroup.com/sites/default/files/asset/document/Syracuse_gb .pdf.

130 Henry S. Kenyon, "Spacecraft Ties Distant Battlefields into One Network," *Signal*, September 2003, https://www.afcea.org/content/?q=node/155.

131 Telespazio, "Sicral 2," accessed February 19, 2018, 1, www.telespazio.com/documents/9986169/ 43239100/SICRAL2_scheda_eng.pdf.

seven steerable beams, which provide the French military with additional capacity to communicate in the SHF and EHF frequency ranges.[132]

The next generation of French communications satellites are the *Syracuse-4* satellites.[133] These two satellites will help meet the French military's current explosion in satellite communication requirements by providing renewed, additional capability in the SHF frequency range, in the X and Ka bands specifically.[134] This explosion in information requirements is related to an increasing number of French combat systems relying on information exchange, such as jets communicating information between themselves and a command center. All French communication systems are in some way hardened, with the *Syracuse-4* satellites designed to employ anti-jamming antennas and on-board processing, for example. The French military deployed 93 satellite communications ground stations in all the locations where French troops were present in 2016.[135]

The French military currently uses both military and civilian signals from GPS, based on an agreement it reached with the U.S. government.[136] As a result of this agreement, most French guided munitions use GPS; only a handful of special missions employing PNT did not use GPS in 2017.[137] The military employs GPS receivers developed in France, as well as GPS receivers purchased from the United States through the U.S. Foreign Military Sales Program. The French will transition to using ESA's Galiléo PNT system more fully over the coming years. The system will employ 30 satellites operating in a medium Earth orbit; its protected PNT services will become available in

---

[132] Peter B. de Selding, "Ariane-5 Lofts Athena-Fidus and ABS's First Built to Order Satellite," *SpaceNews*, February 7, 2014, http://spacenews.com/39410ariane-5-lofts-athena-fidus-and-abss-1st-built-to-order-satellite/.

[133] *French National Assembly*, Breton, 4.

[134] Caleb Henry, "French DGA Orders Two All-Electric Military Satellites as Syracuse III Sucessor," *Via Satellite*, December 23, 2015, http://www.satellitetoday.com/government-military/2015/12/23/french-dga-orders-two-all-electric-military-satellites-as-Syracuse-3-successor/undefined.

[135] *French National Assembly*, Breton, 3.

[136] *French National Assembly*, Testé, 7.

[137] *French National Assembly*, Breton, 3.

2020.[138][139] Faced with an increased threat of jamming in the current operating environment, France plans to use PNT receivers with access to multiple satellite constellations, typically GPS and Galiléo. The United States has made a similar request to the European Commission to access the Galiléo PNT system.[140] Through the so-called OMEGA program, the French military is also actively researching how to implement technical improvements to its receivers to make its high value platforms and munitions more resistant to jamming over the next two years.[141]

In 2009, the French launched two *Spirale* (*Système Préparatoire Infra-Rouge pour l'Alerte*) experimental satellites to develop the technology necessary for an operational missile-warning satellite system.[142] At the time, the French military planned to field an operational missile-warning satellite system in the 2019 timeframe.[143] However, the timeline has been pushed back since 2009. This delay may be due in part to concerns that France's European partners and the United States have expressed in the past about its plans to develop a missile-warning satellite system in addition to the aforementioned funding constraints.[144][145] The CIE commandant reported that the military would be studying the issue of advanced missile warning again with funds from the 2020–2024 LPM.[146]

As discussed in the first section of this chapter, France is working to improve its SSA network, including its GRAVES tracking radar. The GRAVES radar is presently capable of tracking objects .1 m in size at distances of up to 200 km and objects 1 m in size

[138] ESA, "What is Galiléo?," accessed February 19, 2018, http://www.esa.int/Our_Activities/Navigation/Galileo/What_is_Galileo.

[139] *French National Assembly*, Testé, 7.

[140] *French National Assembly*, Testé, 14.

[141] *French National Assembly*, Testé, 7.

[142] Peter B. de Selding, "French Spirale Satellites to Continue Mission-detection Test Mission thru End of Year," *Space News*, June 21, 2010, http://spacenews.com/french-spirale-satellites-continue-missile-detection-test-mission-through-end-year/.

[143] Heisbourg and Pasco, *Espace Militaire*, 103.

[144] SpaceNews Staff, "French Joint Space Command on Schedule to Open in July," *SpaceNews*, April 25, 2010, http://spacenews.com/french-joint-space-command-schedule-open-july/.

[145] Heisbourg and Pasco, *Espace Militaire*, 103.

[146] *French National Assembly*, Testé, 8.

at 1,000 km.[147][148] The military wants to improve GRAVES' capability from being able to track objects 1 m in size to tracking objects .5 m in size at the same distance by 2025. Improvements beyond .5 m resolution will require the development of another radar system, presumably one that does not use GRAVES' bi-static design.[149]

The Space Surveillance Division (Division Surveillance de l'Espace) of the Air Defense and Air Operations Command is responsible, overall, for tracking foreign reconnaissance satellites, notably for operational and strategic forces, and for GPS analysis related to the use of precision-guided munitions and search and rescue operations.[150] The Space Surveillance Division carries out five functions in support of this mission: surveillance of low Earth orbit using the GRAVES radar; daily collection and analysis of satellite orbital data; precision satellite tracking using the SATAM (Système d'Acquisition et de Trajectographie des Avions et des Munitions) radars; surveillance of the geostationary arc using the nascent Oscegeane (Observation Spectrale et Caractérisation des Satellites Géostationnaires) telescope / spectroscopy application; and monitoring of space weather using the FEDOME (Fedération des Données de Météorologie de l'Espace) network. Approximately 30 Space Surveillance Division personnel operate France's space situational awareness network at a consolidated space tracking center located near Lyon-Mont Verdun Air Base.[151] The French military maintains access to additional SSA assets, such as TAROT (Télescope à Action Rapide pour les Objets Transitoires) and the Monge

---

147 Jean-Daniel Testé, "SSA: first priority of French military space policy 2025," March 2015, www.jsforum.or.jp/stableuse/2016/pdf/15.%20Teste.pdf, 11. Based on an assessment conducted by the Federation on American Scientist on a similar radar, the GRAVES radar can track one meter objects at a much higher altitude. See Federation of American Scientists, "A Graves Sourcebook," August 7, 2013, https://fas.org/spp/military/ program/track/graves.pdf,1.

148 *French National Assembly*, Breton, 7.

149 H. Klinkrad, "Monitoring Space – Efforts Made by European Countries," accessed March 1, 2018, http://www.fas.org/spp/military/program/track/klinkrad.pdf

150 Ministère des Armées, "Division Surveillance de l'Espace du Commandement de la Défense Aérienne et des Operations Aériennes," March 20, 2012, https://www.defense.gouv.fr/english/actualites/ dossiers/l-espace-au-profit-des-operations-militaires/fiches-techniques/dse-cdaoa [translated by the author].

151 Amy Svitak, "EU Aims for Space Situational Awareness Network," *Aviation Week*, August 5, 2013, http:// aviationweek.com/awin/eu-aims-space-situational-awareness-network.

tracking ships, which appear to be employed as supporting sensors to the Space Surveillance Division network.[152]

Since the late 1980s, the French military has not needed to maintain independent satellites for terrestrial weather because the European Organisation for the Exploitation of Meteorological Satellites (EUMETSAT) and its international partners could provide it with weather updates.[153] Although EUMETSAT has partnered with the Department of Defense in the past, it is ultimately an intergovernmental organization rather than a French organization.[154][155] It currently operates eight weather satellites in various orbits.[156]

CNES launches French military satellites from the Guiana Space Center (Centre Spatial Guyanais). The Guiana Space Center is located at five degrees of latitude, making it an efficient location for launching satellites into a geostationary into orbit.[157] The Guiana Space Center is co-operated by ESA and CNES.[158]

French military satellites are currently launched on Ariane-5 rockets developed by the ESA.[159] The Ariane-5 is capable of putting a 10-ton payload into a geosynchronous transfer orbit or a 19-ton payload into a low Earth orbit, at 500 km altitude. ESA will transition to using the Ariane-6 rocket to launch their satellites during years of 2020–

---

[152] For a more complete list and locations of these assets, see Testé, "SSA: first priority," 10. See also Gosnold, "Hearing of the French Joint Commander for Space," *Satellite Observation*, February 5, 2018, https://satelliteobservation.wordpress.com/2018/02/05/hearing-of-the-french-joint-commander-for-space/.

[153] "The Emerging European Military Space Capability," *Strategic Comments*, vol. 2, no. 3 (1996), 1 https://doi.org/10.1080/1356788960233.

[154] NASA, "Aeronautics and Space Report of the President: Department of Defense (DoD)," 1997, https://history. nasa.gov/presrp97/dod.htm.

[155] Bloomberg Markets, "Company Overview of European Organization for the Exploitation of Meteorological Satellites," *Bloomberg*, accessed March 1, 2018, https://www.bloomberg. com/research/stocks/private/snapshot.asp? privcapId=8597933.

[156] EUMETSAT, "Current Satellites," accessed February 20, 2018, https://www.eumetsat.int/website/home/Satellites/CurrentSatellites/index.html.

[157] ESA, "Europe's Space Port," May 3, 2017, https://www.esa.int/Our_Activities/Space_Transportation/Europe_s_ Spaceport/Europe_s_Spaceport2.

[158] ESA, "ESA and CNES Sign Contract on CSG," May 2, 2002, http://www.esa.int/Our_Activities/Space_Transportation/ESA_and_CNES_sign_contract_on_CSG.

[159] "Space Launch Report: Ariane 5 Data Sheet," *Space Launch Report*, accessed January 25, 2018, http://www.spacelaunchreport.com/ariane5.html.

2022.[160] The Ariane-6 will be capable of putting a 10-ton payload into a geosynchronous transfer orbit or into lower orbits more affordably than the Ariane-5 rocket can.[161] CNES also employs Soyuz rockets for medium lift and Véga rockets for small lift requirements.[162]

D.   ANALYSIS

Part 4 analyzes the preceding three parts of this chapter to develop an understanding of how the U.S. Department of Defense might come to benefit from closer military space collaboration with the French Defense Ministry. This analysis is continued in chapter 5, when similarities and differences can be drawn among French, Australian, and Japanese space activities.

Based on part A, the United States has benefitted from the French desire to promote responsible behavior in space since 2008. Beginning in 2008, France pushed for the Code of Conduct for Outer Space Activities, which the United States eventually rallied behind. Although the proposal fell apart under pressure, most notably, from China and Russia, France and the United States occupied a common diplomatic front for a time as they tried to advance this common cause. Along the same lines as the code of conduct, France and the United States have signed information-sharing agreements for SSA data in recent years. This has contributed to the United States and France developing common situational awareness about activities in space and building consensus. Gaining access to the French SSA sensors should permit the United States to calculate the ephemeris data of space objects more accurately.

Based on part B, the United States military has benefited from the commercial orientation of French space activities. The U.S. Air Force and Army exploited imagery from French commercial satellites beginning in the early 1990s. The U.S. government currently shares commercial satellite imagery with its international partners thanks to the

---

160 Caleb Henry, "Ariane 5 down to two dozen launches before Ariane 6 takes over," *Space News*, January 16, 2018, http://spacenews.com/ariane-5-down-to-two-dozen-launches-before-ariane-6-takes-over/ (accessed March 2, 2018).

161 ESA, "Ariane 6," July 12, 2017, https://www.esa.int/Our_Activities/Space_Transportation/Launch_vehicles/ Ariane_6.

162 CNES, "La France célèbre," 2.

security benefits and additional capacity that commercial imagery offers. The U.S. government would not have moved to commercial imagery exploitation as early as it did had the French not commercialized the *SPOT* images in the 1980s.

Similarly, France's decision to commercialize Ariane launchers could benefit the United States more than it has to date. However, the U.S. government launches its payloads exclusively on the rockets of U.S. launch providers, meaning that the free market is not truly at work driving down prices. The French government is also not benefiting financially from the current success of SpaceX. Instead, it is funding the development of the Ariane 6 launcher and providing preferential treatment to Arianespace in the hope of making the Ariane launcher more viable. Upon reflection, the United States and France may find that they can pursue policies that protect their financial interests and the viability of their preferred launch providers for government payloads but allow for more flexibility in the selection of launch providers. Perhaps this could result in Arianespace launching a U.S. government payload to geosynchronous orbit out of the Guiana Space Center under the right conditions or in the French using SpaceX.

Based on part C, the Department of Defense could benefit from several additional French space related capabilities in addition to the ones discussed above. France's Earth imaging satellites do not produce a large number of images each day. Nevertheless, the resolution of the French satellite images is consistent with the resolution of the best commercially available imagery and useful for military purposes. By gaining greater access to French surveillance satellites, the U.S. military makes it more difficult for our adversaries to avoid being imaged. Bringing the French into the planned Combined Space Operations Center, which is discussed more in chapter 3, will aid with this type of tasking.

French ELINT satellite capabilities would complement U.S. ELINT capabilities as well. There is not a well-developed commercial market for satellite ELINT. Furthermore, French ELINT satellites are likely to collect on a wider range of frequencies than commercial automatic identification systems do, for instance.

France's military SATCOM is NATO compatible, which would facilitate U.S. forces communicating over French SATCOM and provide some redundancy to U.S.

systems. However, France appears to have a shortfall in military satellite bandwidth. Furthermore, French interest is centered over Europe, Africa, and Eurasia. These limitations could work to the advantage of the United States financially if France was to buy into a U.S. government owned worldwide constellation, such as *Wideband Global SATCOM* (*WGS*) as a result.

The United States has belatedly recognized the benefit of European development of an independent PNT constellation, in Galileo. The existence of another constellation complicates adversary jamming by increasing the frequency range of the PNT satellites. Furthermore, a second PNT constellation provides redundancy in the event that GPS experiences system downtime.

France is currently studying how to gain access to better missile-warning satellite information. The quality of the missile warning data that the U.S. provides to all NATO countries appears to be unsatisfactory for tactical operations.[163] Therefore, the United States may find it beneficial to provide the French military with access to better missile warning data if it increases France's battlefield lethality.

---

[163] Heisbourg and Pasco, *Espace Militaire*, 103.

III. AUSTRALIA

This chapter on Australian military space activities has four parts. The first part describes the strategic direction of Australia's military space efforts and touches upon the significance of collaboration in space to the U.S.-Australian security alliance. The second part describes briefly the origins of Australia's military space efforts and historical military space collaboration between the United States and Australia. The third part describes the organization and capabilities of Australia's military space efforts. The last part analyzes the preceding three parts to present the areas in which the United States Department of Defense might benefit from closer military space collaboration with the Australian Department of Defence.

A. STRATEGIC DIRECTION AND PREDISPOSITION TO COLLABORATE

Part A presents a series of developments that have affected Australian military space activities from World War II to the present. These developments include the founding of the Woomera test range, the launch of Australia's first satellite, the establishment of joint Australian-U.S. space research facilities on Australian soil, and recent efforts to ground the country's civil and military space initiatives within a coherent and sustainable national framework.

In 1951, Australia and the United States signaled a shared commitment to one another by signing the Security Treaty among Australia, New Zealand, and the United States (ANZUS). The ANZUS treaty helped to address U.S. government concern with the spread of communism in Asia and Australian government concern with a resurgent Japan.[164] As part of the treaty, the United States and Australia resolved that when the "territorial integrity, political independence or security of any of the Parties is threatened

---

164 Christopher Hubbard, *Australian and U.S. Military Cooperation: Fighting Common Enemies* (Burlington, VT: Ashgate, 2005), 3–4.

in the Pacific," each party would "act to meet the common danger in accordance with its constitutional processes."[165]

The pledge of mutual support in the ANZUS Treaty was weaker than the pledge of mutual support in the North Atlantic Alliance Treaty. However, the bond between the United States and Australia has been stronger than that shared between the United States and most of its NATO allies. The secret agreements on signals intelligence shared by the United States and Australia have been a major reason for this strong bond.

In 1940, prior to the United States' entry into World War II, the British and United States governments began to cooperate closely in the collection and sharing of signals intelligence.[166] These two governments reaffirmed their desire for close cooperation in the collection and sharing of signals intelligence in the 1946 British-U.S. Communications Intelligence Agreement. In 1948, Canada, Australia, and New Zealand became party to the 1946 British-U.S. Communications Intelligence Agreement pending formal assurance that they would abide by the terms of it.[167]

In *Asia's Space Race*, Clay Moltz writes that space activity in Australia has historically been linked to the United Kingdom's early missile program and the United States' civil, intelligence related, and military space activities.[168] British involvement in the country stemmed from Australia's status as a British Dominion and then as a Commonwealth State. From 1946 until 1980, the British and Australian governments collaborated in the Anglo-Australian Joint Project.[169] This project led to the founding and development of the Long Range Weapons Establishment and the huge Woomera weapons

165 Department of External Affairs, *Security Treaty between Australia, New Zealand and the United States of America [ANZUS]*, September 1, 1951, 1, http://www.austlii.edu.au/au/other/dfat/treaties/1952/2.html.

166 National Security Agency, "UKUSA Agreement Release: 1940–1956," June 24, 2010, https://www.nsagov/news-features/declassified-documents/ukusa/.

167 National Security Agency, "Appendices to U.S.—British Communication Intelligence Agreement," March 5, 1946, 54, https://www.nsa.gov/news-features/declassified-documents/ukusa/assets/files/ appendices_jul48.pdf.

168 James Clay Moltz, *Asia's Space Race: National Motivations, Regional Rivalries, and International Risks* (New York: Columbia University Press, 2011), 160.

169 National Archives of Australia, "Defence research and the Anglo-Australian Joint Project," accessed March 19, 2018, http://guides.naa.gov .au/records-about-south-australia/chapter15/15.4.aspx.

test range in central Australia in 1947.[170] In 1955, the Long Range Weapons Establishment merged with several other defense facilities to form the Weapons Research Establishment (WRE), which would later collaborate with the U.S. Department of Defense on a number of projects.[171]

The Woomera Range Complex provided the space needed for British and Australian testing of the Blue Streak missile in the late 1950s.[172] The Australian and British governments would find the liquid-fueled Blue Streak missile unsuitable for its intended military purpose by 1960. To help justify its expenses on the failed missile program, the British government wanted to transition the missile program into a civilian-oriented rocket program. Great Britain's promotion of the Blue Streak served as the foundation for a European satellite launcher program, contributing significantly to the founding of ELDO in 1961.[173]

Australia benefited from Great Britain's promotion of the Blue Streak to become the only non-European member of ELDO. Its membership was facilitated by the absence of a European spaceport prior to the development of the Guiana Space Center. Early variants of the Europa rockets were launched from the Woomera Range Complex. Moreover, military and civilian work on the Blue Streak program saw well over 1,000 local support staff assisting British and other European rocket engineers working at Woomera through 1967.[174]

In 1967, a joint project among the United Kingdom, Australia, and the United States would launch Australia into the space age. Project SPARTA (Special Antimissile Research Tests, Australia) scientists and engineers used modified Redstone missiles that they launched from the Woomera Range Complex during 1966 and 1967 to observe how various

---

[170] Australian Government Department of Defence, "About the Woomera Prohibited Area," accessed March 19, 2018, http://www.defence.gov. au/woomera/about.htm.

[171] National Library of Australia, "Weapons Research Establishment (Australia) (1955-1978)," accessed March 19, 2018, https://trove.nla.gov .au/people/783674.

[172] The National Archives, "The Blue Streak Rocket," accessed March 19, 2018, http://www. nationalarchives.gov.uk/films/1951to1964/filmpage _rocket.htm.

[173] Sheehan, "European Integration and Space," 77–78.

[174] Moltz, Asia's Space Race, 161.

43

warheads reentered into the Earth's atmosphere.[175] After its first nine launches were successful, Project SPARTA was about to conclude with an unused modified Redstone rocket. The Australians seized the opportunity offered by the unused Redstone to develop and launch the Weapons Research Establishment Satellite.[176] Launched in November 1967, the Weapons Research Establishment Satellite transmitted signals to Earth for five days and carried four scientific experiments on it.[177] NASA would launch the Australian developed amateur radio satellite *OSCAR-5* (*Orbiting Satellite Carrying Amateur Radio-5*) in early 1970. Australia would repeat the feat of developing its own satellites again only in 2002, with Federation Satellite, and in 2017, with a university developed cube satellite.[178]

In 1981, the Australian government and Australia's major telecommunications provider Telecom formed Aussat.[179] The purpose of Aussat was to provide communications across Australia via a domestic satellite network, for both military and commercial usage.[180] Hughes Corporation built the first three Aussat satellites in the United States. The first two Aussat satellites were launched from U.S. space shuttles in 1985.

In 1991, foreign investors, including the American-owned BellSouth Corporation agreed to purchase the debt-ridden Aussat company from its Australian owners.[181] This led to the establishment of the Optus Corporation in 1992. Singapore Telecommunications

---

[175] Andrew J. Lepage, "Old Reliable: The story of the Redstone," *The Space Review*, May 2, 2011, http://www. thespacereview.com/article/1836/1.

[176] Paul Culliver, "50 years since Australia's first satellite, WRESAT, launched from Australia," *Australian Broadcasting Corporation*, November 28, 2017, http://www.abc.net.au/news/2017-11-29/50-years-since-first-satellite-launch-wresat/9205878.

[177] Gunter Dirk Krebs, "Wresat," *Gunter's Space Page*, accessed March 19, 2018, http://space. skyrocket.de/doc_sdat/wresat.htm.

[178] Phys.org, "Australian satellite in orbit," May 26, 2017, https://phys.org/news/2017-05-australian-satellite-orbit.html.

[179] "Aussat: Dawn of TV's Satellite Age," *Television.au*, August 27, 2015, http://televisionau.com/2015/08/aussat-dawn-of-tvs-satellite-age.html.

[180] "Singtel Optus Australia," *Skybrokers*, accessed April 6, 2018, http://www.sky-brokers.com/home/services/satelite-operators/singtel-optus-australia.

[181] Barton Crockett, "Aussie gov't gives Optus nod to set up new carriers; BellSouth, Cable & Wireless to head up effort," *Network World*, December 2, 1991, LexisNexis Academic.

currently owns and operates the third and fourth generations of Optus satellites, which provide commercial and some military communication bandwidth to Australia.[182]

Part of the reason for Australia's lack of vision and independence until recently with regard to space has to do with the United States. An influential author of several works concerning U.S. intelligence and defense satellite facilities in Australia, Desmond Ball argued in 2001 that the signals intelligence agreements with the United States were the most important international agreements to which Australia was party.[183] Another author, writing on Australian and U.S. military cooperation, punctuated the evolution of the ANZUS security treaty over its first 50 years with discussions of the three intelligence gathering and communications facilities established in Australia in the 1960s: North West Cape, Pine Gap, and Nurrungar.[184] Similarly, Brett Biddington, an influential author on Australian space policy, noted in 2008:

> The so-called Joint Defence facilities, notably Pine Gap, near Alice Springs, are regarded as jewels in the crown of Australia's relationship with the United States. The U.S. alliance is the basis of Australia's national strategy. In other words, there is an implicit space component at the heart of Australia's national strategy and national security policy.[185]

Desmond Ball explained the relationship between the Joint Defense space facilities and Australia's security strategy writ large by noting that hosting these joint facilities provided Australia with preferential access to U.S. defense technology, cooperation and exchange agreements, and access to senior strategic councils.[186]

Despite its close security relationship with the United States and to some degree because of it, Australia has struggled to define its own military space policy and program over the years. Brett Biddington explained one reason for this in 2008, when he asked

---

182 "Singtel Optus Australia," *Skybrokers*.

183 Desmond Ball, "The Strategic Essence," *Australian Journal of International Affairs*, vol. 55, no. 2, July 1, 2001, 235.

184 Hubbard, *Australian and U.S. Military Cooperation*, 53.

185 Brett Biddington, "An Australian Perspective on Space Security," in *Collective Security in Space: Asian Perspectives*, ed. John M. Logsdon and James Clay Moltz (The George Washington University, The Elliot School of International Affairs, Space Policy Institute, 2008), 96–97.

186 Ball, "The Strategic Essence," 246.

somewhat rhetorically at that point: "Why should a small nation in population and GDP terms[5] assume technology and risks [of developing its own space systems] at potentially considerable cost, when, to this point at least, there has been no compelling reason to do so?"[187] In seeming response, the Australian government has undertaken various efforts to respond this question and increase its military and civilian presence in space since that time.

Since 2008, space has been the subject of many high-level reviews and policy statements made by the Australian government. The Australian Senate's Standing Committee on Economics as well as the Department of Industry, Innovation and Science have contributed significantly to this increased policy focus. The Department of Defence has similarly elevated the importance of space security at the national level, as evidenced in the three defense white papers that it has produced over the last 10 years.

In 2008, the Australian Senate's Standing Committee on Economics authored a report entitled *Lost in Space?* In submissions to the report, the Commonwealth Scientific and Industrial Research organization stated that it had already spent 100 million Australian dollars on the civil-oriented Square Kilometre Array radio telescope; while the Bureau of Meteorology indicated that it contributed 100 million Australian dollars annually for access to weather data.[188] For its part, the Department of Defence stated that it would spend 927 million Australian dollars for its contribution to the U.S. Wideband Global SATCOM constellation and that it had incurred long-term expenses of over a billion dollars on the space-related Jindalee over-the-horizon Radar. These sums represented a significant investment in space, with the money often going to foreign service providers in exchange for space data.

Overall, the *Lost in Space?* report focused on the state of the country's space science and industry sector and noted a number of false starts for programs that had been

---

187 Biddington, "An Australian Perspective," 97.

.188 Standing Committee on Economics, *Lost in Space? Setting a new direction for Australia's space science and industry sector*, Commonwealth of Australia, November 12, 2008, 49–52, https://www.aph.gov .au/Parliamentary_Business/Committees/Senate/Economics/Completed_inquiries/2008-10/space_08/report/ index.

aimed at creating a coherent and consolidated national space policy for Australia. These included the failure of the National Space Program (1986-2001), the failure of the Australian Space Office (1987-1995), and the failure of the Cooperative Research Centre for Satellite Systems (1998-2004), among other initiatives.[189] Given the transience of the government's previous efforts, the standing committee who authored the report recommended that the government make a gradual evolution toward a new national space agency.[190] As part of this evolution, the report called for the establishment of a Space Industry Advisory Council comprised of representatives from industry, government agencies, the Department of Defence, and academics.

In 2009, the Australian Department of Defence released its first white paper in nine years. Unsurprisingly, the review recognized that space systems had grown increasingly important to military operations in the intervening period.[191] The report further recognized that attacks on critical space systems were a rising threat to Australia and the United States.[192] The review announced plans to develop space specialists within the Department of Defence. The government also announced plans to purchase a remote sensing satellite in the review, which it said would add to Australia's standing as a contributing partner to the U.S. space efforts.[193] The planned satellite appears to have eventually manifested itself in Defence Project 799, announced eight years later, in June 2017.[194]

By the middle of 2009, the Australian government had established the Space Policy Unit within the Department of Innovation, Industry, Science, and Research and mandated that the unit bring forward a national space industry policy.[195] The government released its

---

[189] Standing Committee on Economics, *Lost in Space*, 44–45

[190] Standing Committee on Economics, *Lost in Space*, 66.

[191] Department of Defence, *Defending Australia in the Asia Pacific Century: Force 2030*, May 2, 88, 2009, http://www. defence.gov.au/whitepaper/2009/.

[192] Department of Defence, Defending Australia in the Asia Pacific Century, 88.

[193] Department of Defence, Defending Australia in the Asia Pacific Century, 82.

[194] Department of Defence, "Defence Project 799: Enhanced Satellite ISR Capability," accessed March 24, 2018, http://www.defence.gov.au/ AGO/geoint-def799-satellites.htm.

[195] International Astronautical Federation, "Space Coordination Office, Department of Industry," accessed March 24, 2018, http://www. iafastro.org/societes/space-coordination-office-department-of-industry/.

Principles for a National Space Industry Policy in 2011. Nevertheless, the previously mandated National Space Industry Policy seemed to have mutated into the nominally less consequential *State of Space* report in the next several years.

In 2013, the Department of Defence released a second white paper. The review's introduction highlighted the lingering effects of the global financial crisis and the U.S. pivot toward Pacific as two changes to the strategic environment.[196] The 2013 review placed greater emphasis on the U.S. Alliance than the 2009 review had. Two subsections in the report were devoted to space and communications cooperation with the United States. In the first of these subsections, the review mentions the relocation of a U.S. C-Band radar to the Harold E. Holt Naval Communications Station at Exmouth, as well as planned discussions to relocate a U.S. space surveillance telescope to Australia.[197] Pine Gap is the only joint facility mentioned in the subsection.[198] Tellingly, each time that Pine Gap enters into the discussion of joint facilities in any of the three reviews, be it 2009, 2013, or 2016, it is accompanied by a statement that the Australian government has "full knowledge and concurrence" of the activities that go on there. The review announced the government's intention to continue to grow the number of space-trained personnel across the Defence Department in order to maximize its investments in space and cooperation with the United States.[199]

From 2014 through 2016, the Department of Industry, Innovation and Science released the *State of Space* report annually.[200] The report served as a compendium, summarizing the civilian space-related activities conducted by the Australian government's major departments and other agencies.

---

196 Department of Defence, *Defence White Paper 2013*, May 3, 2013, http://www.defence.gov.au/ whitepaper/2013/, ix-3.

197 Department of Defence, *Defence White Paper 2013*, 57–58.

198 Department of Defence, *Defence White Paper 2013*, 58.

199 Department of Defence, *Defence White Paper 2013*, 81.

200 Department of Industry, Innovation and Science, "The State of Space Report," accessed March 24, 2018, https://www.industry.gov.au/industry/IndustrySectors/space/Publications/Pages/The-State-of-Space-Report.aspx.

In 2016, the Australian government released the results of its third defense white paper in the last 10 years. This was clearly the most ambitious review of the three, and in the words of the Defence Minister, it was "the first Defence White Paper to be fully costed, with external private sector assurance of the White Paper's investment plans."[201] The government announced that it would fund the objectives set out in the review by increasing the defense budget to two percent of Australia's GDP by 2020–2021.

The 2016 white paper saw a rise in non-geographic threats in space as well as differences arising between China and the United States concerning the rules that governed conduct in space as two of the changes to the strategic environment.[202] As a result of increased threats to allied space assets, the Department of Defence reaffirmed its commitment to strengthen Australia's space surveillance and situational awareness through the relocation of the U.S. optical telescope to the Harold E. Holt Communications Facility, supported by planned upgrades to the facility.[203] The Department of Defence planned, additionally, to increase its intelligence and targeting capacity through increased access to allied and commercial assets and, potentially, through increased investment in space-based sensors.[204] It planned similarly to continue increasing the number of uniformed and civilian personnel working in space-related functions.[205]

Finally, in 2017, in a move welcomed by government and industry officials, Australia's Minister of Education announced the government's plan to establish a national space agency.[206] The government had created a working group, led by a former head of CSIRO, to advise it on the scope and structure of the agency at the time of the

---

[201] Department of Defence, *2016 Defence White Paper*, February 25, 2016, 9, http://www.defence.gov .au/whitepaper/.

[202] Department of Defence, *2016 Defence White Paper*, 16 and 43.

[203] Department of Defence, *2016 Defence White Paper*, 87 and 104.

[204] Department of Defence, *2016 Defence White Paper*, 87.

[205] Department of Defence, *2016 Defence White Paper*, 43 and 147.

[206] Jeff Foust, "Australia to establish a national space agency," *Space News*, September 24, 2017, http://spacenews.com/australia-to-establish-national-space-agency/. The time difference between Australia and other countries appears to have resulted in the September 25th announcement in Australia being report on September 24th elsewhere.

announcement.[207] The working group was initially supposed to provide its recommendations to the government by the end of March 2018. Although the recommendations were not forthcoming by the end of March, it is perhaps noteworthy, in pursuit of this effort, that Boeing and CSIRO had announced a long-term partnership aimed at exploring the potential for space infrastructure development and market related research and development in Australia by the end of January 2018.[208]

B.   HISTORICAL COLLABORATION

Part B briefly describes the origins of Australia military space efforts and historical collaboration between the United States and Australia in space across military, civilian, and commercial entities. It shows the effects of previous U.S. policy decisions governing the U.S. presence in Australia and how the joint space research facilities and associated capabilities came to exist there. This information is relevant when considering the strength and limitations of military collaboration in space with Australia, shaping future policy decisions.

While the Australian government's capability to develop and launch a satellite improved from the late 1940s until the late 1960s, as presented in the previous section, Australia's location in the opposite hemisphere of the globe to the United States and its remote and well-protected locations encouraged the development of U.S. government telemetry and tracking stations in Australia beginning in the mid-to-late 1950s. The U.S. government began making plans to build tracking stations for the Vanguard satellite program in 1955.[209] Construction of the stations was led by the Army Corps of Engineers,

---

[207] Steven Trask, "Government Announces Creation of National Space Agency," *The Canberra Times*, September 26, 2017, http://www.canberratimes.com.au/technology/sci-tech/government-announces-creation-of-national-space-agency-20170924-gynx3c.html?_ga=2.235353091.385887290.1521838567-1793460573.1521838567.

[208] Australian Aviation, "Boeing, CSIRO Announce New Space Partnership," January 29, 2018, australianaviation.com.au/2018/01/boeing-csiro-announce-new-space-partnership/.

[209] Sunny Tsiao, *Read You Loud and Clear! : The Story of NASA's Tracing and Data Flight Network*, NASA, 2008, 15, https://ntrs.nasa.gov/search.jsp?R=20080020389.

which incorporated stations at Woomera and Muchea into the network in October 1957.[210] The U.S. Air Force and Navy linked the Australian Minitrack stations to a control center in the United States via their teletype networks within a few months of the stations' establishment.[211]

The Minitrack network was turned over to NASA after NASA's establishment in 1958.[212] In the 1960s, The WRE ran tracking sites at Carnarvon, Perth, and Woomera in support of NASA's Manned Space Flight Network in the 1960s.[213] NASA historian Sunny Tsaio explains of the Woomera site: "Under agreement with the Australian government, the DOS supplied the land, power, facilities, and workers. In return, the United States furnished all the technical equipment, trained the WRE personnel, and installed the initial equipment."[214] NASA's presence in Australia appears to have evolved over the years under a similar model. Since 1965, a station located in Tidbinbilla, near Canberra, has contributed to NASA's Deep Space Network, and the Australian Government's Commonwealth Scientific and Industrial Research Organization (CSIRO) currently operates one of NASA's three-global Deep Space Network complexes in its entirety.[215] Ninety staff working in Tidbinbilla at the Canberra Deep Space Communications Complex support operations of the station's four 34-meter antennas and one 70-meter antenna.[216] Along with NASA's two other Deep Space Network complexes, located in California and Spain, the Australian complex permits NASA to maintain 24-hour communications with its operational spacecraft.[217]

---

[210] William R. Corliss, "NASA Technical report CR 140390, Histories of the Space Tracking and Data Acquisition Network (STADAN), the Manned Space Flight Network (MSFN), and the NASA Communications Network (NASCOM)," NASA, 1974, https://ntrs.nasa.gov/archive/nasa/casi.ntrs.nasa.gov/19750002909.pdf.

[211] Corliss, "NASA Technical report," 265.

[212] Tsaio, *Read You Loud*, 31.

[213] Tsaio, *Read You Loud*, 114.

[214] Tsaio, *Read You Loud*, 21.

[215] CSIRO, "About Canberra Deep Space Communications Complex," accessed March 25, 2018, https://www.csiro.au/en/ResearchFacilities/CDSCC/About-CDSCC.

[216] CSIRO, "About Canberra Deep Space Communications Complex," accessed March 25, 2018https://www.csiro.au/en/Research/Facilities/CDSCC/About-CDSCC.

[217] Tsaio, *Read You Loud*, xiii.

The Department of Defense has also maintained a continuous presence in Australia since at least 1962. In that year, the U.S. Navy established a station in Australia to communicate with its *Polaris* ballistic missile submarines operating in the Western Pacific Ocean.[218] Among the US-Australian joint facilities, U.S. operations at North West Cape were especially controversial given that, according to Desmond Ball, "Australia had no control over or even any right to be informed about the communications passing through the station, including possible commands to launch nuclear missiles."[219] Many Australians worried that the presence of this station on Australian soil increased the country's exposure to the threat of a nuclear attack. U.S. Naval Communication Station North West Cape was renamed U.S. Naval Communications Station Harold E. Holt in 1968.[220] Some 400 Australians and 525 American personnel were employed at the station in the late 1960s.[221]

The United States augmented Harry E. Holt communications station with satellite communications facilities in the 1970s and 1980s.[222] In 1982, *Polaris* submarines were retired from the Pacific, although the communications station continued to support operations for U.S. attack submarines thereafter. In 1992, the station was turned over to the Royal Australian Navy, who appear to have essentially vacated it by 2002, at which time the majority of personnel assigned to the base were civilian contractors.[223]

In 1965, American engineers reportedly began surveying Pine Gap valley, near Alice Springs, Australia, in order to establish a satellite ground facility there.[224] In late 1966, the Australian government announced that it had signed an agreement with the American Defense Advanced Research Projects Agency for the establishment of the Joint Defence Space Research Facility at Pine Gap. The facility became operational in 1970 and

---

218 Ball, "The Strategic Essence," 237.

219 Ball, "The Strategic Essence," 238.

220 Ball, *A Suitable Piece*, 52.

221 Department of the Environment and Energy, "Naval Communication Station Harold E Holt (Area A), Exmouth, WA, Australia," accessed April 5, 2018, http://www.environment.gov.au/cgi-bin/ahdb/search.pl?mode=place_detail;place_id=103552.

222 Ball, "The Strategic Essence," 238.

223 Department of the Environment, "Naval Communication Station Harold E Holt."

224 Ball, *A Suitable Piece*, 58–65.

has been responsible for communications with various defense and intelligence satellites over the years. By 1978, the facility employed over 450 people, roughly half of whom were Australian. However, at the time, the Top Secret section of the facility was thought to be manned almost entirely by Americans.[225]

In 2001, Desmond Ball estimated that the number of people employed at the Pine Gap facility had nearly doubled to 875 over the previous year, in 2000.[226] A rough parity in numbers was then maintained between Australian and American personnel. This increase in personnel since the 1970s was reportedly accompanied by an increase in direct Australian utilization of the facility, as personnel had begun to relay information back to their headquarters in Canberra and Sydney.

The United States and Australia reached an agreement to establish the Defence Space Communication Station, also known as Nurrungar, in 1969.[227] The erstwhile facility was located within the Woomera restricted area, whose natural advantages have been discussed. In part, financial considerations motivated the decision to build another ground station in Australia, in addition to Pine Gap, as it enabled the U.S. Air Force to employ a single satellite in geostationary orbit, as opposed to two satellites in Molniya orbits, to detect Soviet ICBM launches.[228]

That the facility was a ground station for an early warning satellite program, later known as DSP, would not be announced until the 1980s.[229][230] Furthermore, Jeffrey Richelson states that:

> [Australian prime minister] Gorton's announcement that the United States would be establishing another major facility in Australia (in addition to the facilities at Pine Gap and Northwest Cape for intelligence and communications, respectively), along with the secrecy surrounding it,

---

[225] Ball, *A Suitable Piece*, 65.

[226] Ball, "The Strategic Essence," 240.

[227] Ball, *A Suitable Piece*, 65.

[228] Jeffrey T. Richelson, *America's Space Sentinels: DSP Satellites and National Security* (Lawrence, Kansas: University of Kansas Press, 1999), 49.

[229] Richelson, *America's Space Sentinels*, 50.

[230] Matt Coleman, "Inside Nurrungar," *Australian Broadcasting Corporation*, September 16, 1999, http://www.abc.net.au/pm/stories/ s52512.htm.

would result in the new facility being subject to political controversy in Australia for the next three decades.[231]

By the end of 1971, 519 personnel were assigned to Nurrangar. Over two-thirds of these individuals were American.[232]

After the DSP proved its worth tactically by tracking tactical missiles launched during operation Desert Storm, Australian personnel at Nurrungar began working on the direct applications of the satellite constellation to Australia's defense.[233] This work included the Down Under Early-warning Experiment Exercise in 1997, which successfully combined DSP and the Jindalee over-the-horizon radar to detect anti-ship missiles launched off Australia's northwest coast. In 1999, Nurrungar closed, and DSP operations were then reassigned to a smaller staff using more modern equipment at Pine Gap.[234]

Australia became directly involved in the development of GPS in the 1980s, sending an Australian representative to the program office in 1982.[235] Australia was a lead nation in the testing of the system thanks to its location in the southern hemisphere. After NATO, Australia was the first individual country to establish access to GPS's Precise Positioning Signal.

Moving into the 2000s, the Australian Department of Defence and the U.S. Navy agreed to establish a joint ground station in support of the U.S. Navy's Mobile User Objective System satellite constellation in 2005.[236] A Mobile User Objective System ground station was thereby established near Geraldton, West Australia. This made the Australian Defence Communications Station one of three joint facilities hosted by

---

[231] Richelson, *America's Space Sentinels*, 51.

[232] Richelson, *America's Space Sentinels*, 55.

[233] Ball, "The Strategic Essence," 242.

[234] Coleman, "Inside Nurrungar."

[235] Air Power Development Centre, "Evolution of Australian Military Space," *Pathfinder: Air Power Development Bulletin*, iss. 105, February 2009, 1–2.

[236] Department of Defence, "MOU Signed for Australia-US Joint Military Communication Ground Station," August 11, 2007, https://archive.is/20121127003933/http://www.defence.gov.au/media/DepartmentalTpl.cfm?CurrentId=7242#selection-509.59-509.148.

Australia in 2007, along with the Joint Defence Facility Pine Gap and the Joint Geological and Geophysical Research Station, also located near Alice Springs.[237]

During the Australia-United States Ministerial Consultations in 2010, the defense chiefs from the two countries signed an SSA partnership statement, reflecting significant current interest in this mission area.[238] The statement laid the groundwork among the two defense departments for establishing additional sensors in Australia to track space objects moving over the Asia- Pacific region. The consultations also included discussions on establishing a civil space cooperation framework agreement. Presumably, these discussions will resume following Australia's announcement in 2017 that it will establish a civil space program.

In 2013, the Australia and U.S. defense departments entered into an advanced SSA agreement, which was the first of its kind for the United States.[239] The agreement permitted Australia to make specific requests to the U.S. Strategic Command Joint Space Operations Center for information including maneuver planning, on-orbit anomaly resolution, and electromagnetic spectrum interference reporting and resolution. Given the similarities in the areas of cooperation, there is a discernable continuum from the basic SSA agreement that the Department of Defense signs, to the advanced SSA agreement, and on to the CSpO initiative and the proposed Combined Space Operations Center.

C.   CURRENT MILITARY SPACE ORGANIZATION AND CAPABILITIES

Part C describes the organization and capabilities of Australia's military space activities. This description starts by introducing Australia's first dedicated military space

---

[237] "Australia-US Joint Facility to Be Hosted at Geraldton," *Defense-Aerospace*, February 15, 2007, http://www. defense-aerospace.com/articles-view/release/3/78992/australia-agrees-to-host-new-us-satcom-facility.html.

[238] Department of Foreign Affairs and Trade, "Joint Statement on space security AUSMIN 2010," accessed April 27, 2018, http://dfat.gov.au/geo/united-states-of-america/ausmin/Pages/joint-statement-on-space-security.aspx.

[239] Aerospace Technology, "US and Australia sign space situational awareness data sharing agreement," April 24, 2013, https://www.aerospace-technology.com/uncategorised/newsus-and-australia-sign-space-situational-awareness-data-sharing-agreement/.

operations unit, Number 1 Remote Sensor Unit. It then turns to discussing Australia's military space capabilities, some of which that unit operates.

The Royal Australian Air Force created Number 1 Radar Surveillance Unit largely to operate the Jindalee radar network in 1992.[240] In 2015, the Royal Australian Air Force renamed Number 1 Radar Surveillance Unit, making it Number 1 Remote Sensor Unit.[241] The name change reflected the importance that remote sensing had assumed for Australia's defense and the increased emphasis Australia was placing on space situational awareness. The unit has since been headed by a Wing Commander in the Royal Australian Air Force. This is an O-5 position. In 2015, the unit had about 110 assigned personnel, many of whom were dual-trained on the use of both the Jindalee over-the-horizon radar and on space systems. Number 1 Remote Sensor Unit operates several systems within Australia's Space Surveillance Network and the Australian Mission Processor, which directly downloads overhead persistent infrared information from the U.S. Air Force's Space Based Infra-red System (SBIRS).[242][243]

Number 1 Remote Sensor Unit is located on Royal Australian Air Force Base Edinburgh.[244] Early in its existence, the base housed the headquarters for the Long Range Weapons Establishment. The base was used almost entirely for activities related to the testing of weapons at Woomera through the 1960s and supported a growing list of activities after that.[245]

A successor to the Weapons Research Establishment, the Defense Science and Technology Group currently maintains an office adjacent to RAAF Edinburgh.[246] Within

[240] Jaimie Abbot, "First Space Operations Unit," *Air Force*, vol. 57, no. 9, May 21, 2015, 12.

[241] Abbot, "First Space Operations," 12.

[242] Elliot, "Joint Force Tracking," 12.

[243] Gene Elliot, "Satellite Monitoring System Comes Online in September," *Air Force*, vol. 57, no. 9, May 21, 2015, http://www.defence.gov.au/Publications/NewsPapers/Raaf/editions/5709a/5709a.pdf, 12.

[244] Gene Elliot, "Joint Force Tracking Items Orbiting Earth," *Air Force*, vol. 57, no. 9, May 21, 2015, http://www.defence.gov.au/Publications/NewsPapers/Raaf/editions/5709a/5709a.pdf, 12.

[245] The Parliament of the Commonwealth of Australia Standing Committee on Public Works, "RAAF Base Edinburgh, Redevelopment Stage 1, Adelaide," October 5, 2000, aph.gov.au.

[246] Department of Defence, "DSTO Edinburgh, South Australia," 2017, 1, http://www.defence.gov.au /id/_Master/docs/NCRP/SA/1073DSTOEdinburghSA.pdf.

its development portfolio, the Defence Science and Technology Group's National Security and Intelligence, Surveillance, and Reconnaissance Division maintains practically all of the systems that Number 1 Remote Sensor Unit operates.[247] The National Security and Intelligence, Surveillance, and Reconnaissance Division is involved in the Square Dance program, in which several space-related government organizations in United States also participate.

This section now turns to discussing Australia's capabilities related to the space-based intelligence, surveillance, and reconnaissance, communications, and space situational awareness mission areas.[248] Australia maintains access to a sizeable number of defense-related foreign-operated space systems in these mission areas, reflecting hundreds of millions of dollars spent on space each year.

In June 2017, the Australian government announced a 500 million Australian dollar investment in the country's intelligence, surveillance, and reconnaissance capabilities as part of Project 799.[249] Project 799 has two phases. In phase one, the Department of Defence has sought to gain more timely and direct access to data from commercial imaging satellites.[250] This has resulted in a 14 million Australian dollar investment in ground stations to download the commercial imagery. In August 2017, the Australian government signed a four-year 104 million Australian dollar (83 million U.S. dollar) contract with DigitalGlobe, too, for access to its imagery library and direct access to its satellites.[251] The

---

[247] Department of Defence: Science and Technology, "National Security and Intelligence, Surveillance, and Reconnaissance Division: Strategic Plan 2016–2020," August 25, 2016, 31 https://www.dst.defence.gov.au/sites/default/files/divisions/documents/National%20Security%20and%20ISR%20S%26T%20Strategy%202016-2020.pdf.

[248] The Department of Defence's access to weather data, PNT, and launch services were touched upon in the first two parts of this chapter. Australia does not maintain or currently appear to be pursuing an autonomous space-related capability in any of these three areas, so they are omitted from discussion in part three.

[249] Department of Defence, "Defence Project 799: Enhanced ISR Capability," accessed April 8, 2018, http://www.defence.gov.au/AGO/ geoint-def799-satellites.htm.

[250] Department of Defence: Strategic Policy and Intelligence, "Defence Project 799," accessed April 8, 2018, http://www.defence.gov.au/ AGO/library/DEF_799_Enhanced_Satellite_ISR_Capability.pdf.

[251] Elizabeth Abbey, "Australian Defence Signs $100 Million Deal for High-res Satellite Imagery," *Spatial Source*, August 22, 2017, https://www.spatialsource.com.au/remote-sensing/australian-defense-signs-100-million-deal-high-res-satellite-imagery.

government announced that it would look into acquiring its own earth imaging satellite in phase two. Although the government has not made the formal decision to acquire its own earth imaging satellite, the Defence Science and Technology's National Security and Intelligence, Surveillance, and Reconnaissance Division's Strategic Plan indicates that the Australian government will invest three to four billion Australian dollars on satellite imagery capability from 2023 through 2035, making this appear likely.[252]

In 2013, the U.S. Air Force awarded Northrop Grumman a 12 million U.S. dollar contract to build Australian Mission Processor Phase 3, also known as Joint Project 2057 Phase 3.[253] The system processes data from SBIRS and DSP satellites in Australia's area of interest. The processor is operated by Number 1 Remote Sensor Unit and managed by the Defence Space Coordinating Office at Air Force Headquarters.[254]

For space-based signals intelligence, the Australian Signals Directorate has a team at the Joint Defence Space Research Facility at Pine Gap.[255] The Australian Signals Directorate held the name of Defence Signals Directorate until 2013, when it was renamed to reflect a whole-of-government approach to signals collection and processing.[256]

Australia employs a mix of dedicated military and commercial SATCOM systems. In 2007, the Australian government reached an agreement with the U.S. government to fund the sixth *WGS* satellite in exchange for gaining communications access to the entire *WGS* constellation through 2026.[257] The *WGS* satellites provide Australia with 2.4 GHz of

---

[252] Department of Defence, "National Security and Intelligence," 31.

[253] SpaceNews Editor, "Missile Warning Data System Ordered for Australia," *Space News*, September 30, 2013, http://spacenews.com/37458missile-warning-data-system-ordered-for-australia/.

[254] Srivari Aishwarya, "Australia's CASG Deliver Battle-space Awareness Capability to RAAF," *Air Force Technology*, August 25, 2016, https://www.airforce-technology.com/uncategorised/newsaustralias-casg-delivers-battle-space-awareness-capability-to-raaf-4989342/.

[255] Tim Leslie and Mark Corcoran, "Explained: Australia's Involvement with the NSA, the U.S. Spy Agency at the Heart of the Global Scandal," *Australia Broadcasting Corporation*, November 18, 2013, http://www.abc.net.au/news/ 2013–11–08/australian-nsa-involvement-explained/5079786.

[256] Department of Defence, "History," accessed April 8, 2018, https://www.asd.gov.au/about/history.htm.

[257] "JP 2008 – Heading for the Projects of Concern List," *Asia-Pacific Defence Reporter*, April 2, 2014, https:// www.asiapacificdefencereporter.com/articles/431/JP-2008-heading-for-the-Projects-of-Concern-list.

secure global military communications in the X and Ka bands.[258] A substantial amount of Australia's total capacity on the *WGS* constellation is centered over the Indian and Pacific Oceans, with less bandwidth provided elsewhere around the globe.[259]

WGS acquisition has been part of a larger Australian satellite communications project known as Joint Project 2008.[260] Unfortunately, Joint Project 2008 has experienced schedule delays and cost overruns. This has been due to issues that Australian Defence Force contractor BAE Systems has experienced while building *WGS* ground stations in southeastern and southwestern Australia, at Harman and Geraldton. This delay has led to throughput constraints within Australia's *WGS* ground stations, affecting military operations and exercises. The Australian Defence Force lacks sufficient *WGS* user terminals as well.

In addition to *WGS*, the Australian Defence Force relies on capacity on *Optus C1*, a hosted ultra-high frequency payload on Intelsat-22, and commercial SATCOM from Inmarsat, ViaSat, and SpeedCast.[261] The Australian government has requested Singtel to remove all commercial customers off of *Optus C1* and to place the satellite into an inclined orbit in order to increase the satellite's usefulness to the Australian military. *Optus C1* is located at 156 degrees East longitude and operates in the Ku band.[262]

In 2019, the Australian government will begin a new SATCOM program called Joint Project 9102. According to the head of Australian Defence Force's Information and Technology Operations, that program will begin to take shape once the U.S. government conducts an analysis of alternatives for its own wideband and narrowband SATCOM.[263]

---

[258] Caleb Henry, "Australia's Military Including Commercial Capacity in Its Satellite Communications Plan," *Space News*, May 22, 2017, http://spacenews.com/australias-military-including-commercial-capacity-in-its-satellite-communications-plans/.

[259] Caleb Henry, "Australian Military Frustrated by Out of Sync Space and Ground Assets," *Space News*, July 3, 2017, http://spacenews.com/australian-military-frustrated-by-out-of-sync-space-and-ground-assets/.

[260] Henry, "Australian Military Frustrated," *Space News*.

[261] Henry, "Australian Military Frustrated," *Space News*.

[262] Singtel Optus Pty Limited, "Optus C1: An Australian Hotbird," accessed April 8, 2018, https://www.optus.com.au/about/ network/satellite/fleet/c1.

[263] Henry, "Australian Military Frustrated." *Space News*.

In 2014, defense officials from Australia, the United States, and Canada signed a Memorandum of Understanding to share data on satellite orbits, methods to mitigate satellite communication interference, GPS accuracy, and space weather data.[264] This Memorandum of Understanding effectively established the CSpO initiative. New Zealand was later brought into the initiative. In March 2018, the Commander of U.S. Strategic Command, General John Hyten, announced that Germany and France would also be included in the CSpO initiative and that a Combined Space Operations Center would be formed by the end of 2018 to facilitate centralized planning and tasking among CSpO initiative partners and decentralized execution.[265]

In 2015, the U.S. government relocated the C-band Space Surveillance Radar to Communications Station Harold E. Holt.[266] The system attained full operational capability in March 2017. The radar provides the United States and Australia with early detection for launches in the southern and eastern hemispheres and improves orbital predictions and positional accuracy for on-orbit objects. The system tracks objects in low-Earth orbit specifically.[267] The U.S. owned radar is operated by Number 1 Remote Sensing Unit personnel located at Royal Australian Air Force Base Edinburgh.[268] Interestingly, the C-band Space Surveillance Radar first entered operations in 1963 at a NASA space tracking station located in western Australia. It was then relocated to Florida and Antigua and now back to Australia.

---

[264] Joey Cheng, "Stratcom Signs Space Data Agreement with U.K., Canada, Australia," *Defense Systems*, September 23, 2014, https://defensesystems.com/articles/2014/09/23/us-multination-space-agreement.aspx.

[265] *Fiscal Year 2019 Budget Request for National Security Space: Hearing before the Armed Services Committee*, Senate, 115th Cong., 2nd sess. (March 20, 2018) (statement of John E. Hyten, Commander, U.S. Strategic Command), 12, 2018, https://www. armed-services.senate.gov/imo/media/doc/Hyten_03-20-18.pdf.

[266] Steve Kotecki, "C-band Radar Reaches Full Operational Capability in Australia," *Peterson Space Observer*, March 7, 2017, http://www.csmng.com/2017/03/17/c-band-radar-reaches-full-operational-capability-in-australia/

[267] Space News Editor, "U.S. Putting Space-tracking Radar, Telescope in Australia," *Space News*, November 16, 2012, http://spacenews.com/us-putting-space-tracking-radar-telescope-in-australia/.

[268] United States Air Force, "1 RSU Space Systems," January 25, 2017, http://www.peterson.af.mil/About/Fact-Sheets/Display/Article/1059617/1-rsu-space-systems/.

In 2016, the U.S. Air Force took over ownership of the Space Surveillance Telescope from the Defence Advanced Research Project Agency.[269] The U.S. and Australian governments agreed in 2013 to relocate the telescope from New Mexico to Australia. Presumably, the move will take place once the Australian government finishes construction on a 63 million Australian dollar facility being built at Communications Station Harold E. Holt to house the telescope.[270] Communications Station Harold E. Holt was selected among potential locations in Australia to house the Space Surveillance Telescope due to its location with regard to objects in geostationary orbit and the monsoonal cloud band. Number 1 Remote Sensor Unit will operate the Space Surveillance Telescope.[271]

D.   ANALYSIS

Part D analyzes the preceding three parts to present the areas in which the U.S. Department of Defense might benefit from closer military space collaboration with the Australian Department of Defence. Based on part A, the Joint Defence Space Research Facility at Pine Gap has helped to solidify the already mutual commitment of the U.S. and Australian defense establishments. Pine Gap's remote, protected location and position in the southern and eastern hemispheres make it ideal for communication with a variety of national satellite payloads. The facility can communicate with satellites operating in geostationary orbits near the longitudinal position of the facility. Furthermore, satellites operating in Molniya orbits tend to make their closest approach to Earth over the southern hemisphere. This proximity would decrease the free space loss of signals transmitted to this facility and similar facilities located in Australia from satellites placed into highly elliptical orbits. Ground stations in somewhat less remote locations in Australia, such as Geraldton, offer similar benefits to the programs they support.

---

[269] Cheryl Pellerin, "DARPA to Transfer Advanced Space Debris Telescope to Air Force," *U.S. Department of Defense*, October 18, 2016, https://www.defense.gov/News/Article/Article/976146/darpa-to-transfer-advanced-space-debris-telescope-to-air-force/.

[270] Parliament of Australia, "Project JP 3029 Phase 2 – Defence Space Surveillance Telescope Facilities Project," September 2014, 7–11, http://www.aph.gov.au/~/media/02%20Parliamentary%20 Business/24%20Committees/244%20Joint%20Committees/PWC/Report%207-2014/Chapter%202. pdf?l=en.

[271] United States Air Force, "1 RSU Space Systems."

Based on part B, Australians have been integral to the operations of U.S. and joint space facilities located in the Australia since at least the 1960s. Nowhere is this more evident than at the Canberra Deep Space Communication Complex, entirely manned by Australians today, although the same can evidently be said for current and planned operations at Naval Communication Station Harold E Holt. The Joint Defence Space Research Facility at Pine Gap is also jointly manned. This likely results in a significant cost savings to the United States government in terms of training and personnel support.

Since the 1990s, the Australian military has sought to integrate Defense Support Program data into its ground-based missile detection network. It is undertaking similar efforts with SBIRS. This integration benefits the United States by making the Australian military more lethal. For instance, better sensor to shooter integration facilitates Australian military efforts to target a missile or a ship firing a missile toward the space research facility at Pine Gap.

Australia's location in the southern hemisphere was a boon to GPS testing. Curiously, the U.S. Air Force also has a contingent of personnel at the Joint Geological and Geophysical Research Station.[272] This would to point toward the continued relevance of Australia's geographic location to ongoing research into the effects of the Earth's magnetic field on air and space systems.

Based on part C, Australia's investment provided the United States with the funds to purchase an additional WGS satellite. In addition to increasing the capacity of the constellation, an additional satellite improves the resiliency of the entire constellation, too, since the WGS satellites can be repositioned to improve system coverage in the event that one or more satellites are inoperable. As noted, Australia is waiting on the United States to conduct an analysis of alternatives for its wideband and narrowband SATCOM, the results of which will inform future Australian investments.

Given that Australia and the United States share the WGS constellation, it follows that the two countries would also want to share information on communication interference

---

272 "Australia-US Joint Facility to Be Hosted at Geraldton," *Defense-Aerospace*.

and space weather, as they do under the CSpO initiative. If the Australian government had its own government-operated satellite, such as the one being discussed under Project 799, that would clearly benefit the operations envisioned at the Combined Space Operations Center, by giving the center an Australian satellite to task.

The once controversial Naval Communication Station Harold E Holt has found a new, relatively benign life as a node of the United States Space Surveillance Network thanks to recent agreements with the Australian government, which will operate the node. The repurposing of NASA's C-band radar as a military radar operated by the Australian Air Force indicates the opportunity for collaboration between non-traditional partners, such as NASA and the Australian Department of Defence or CSIRO and the U.S. Department of Defense, when their interests align.

THIS PAGE INTENTIONALLY LEFT BLANK

IV. JAPAN

Chapter four follows the same format as the previous two chapters, consisting of four parts. Part one presents the security relationship between the Japan and the United States, which has matured slowly, particularly with respect to collaboration in space. Part two discusses the modest collaboration between the civil and military space organizations in the United States and Japan. Part three, on capabilities, highlights Japan's rapidly growing space capabilities, following the release of Japan's first-ever National Security Strategy in 2013. Part four analyzes possible avenues for increased collaboration among defense-related space entities in Japan and the United States.

A.   STRATEGIC DIRECTION AND PREDISPOSITION TO COLLABORATE

As briefly introduced in chapter one, scholars have devoted considerable effort to explaining why Japan's Diet has begun to pass more military-oriented space policies in the past two decades, most especially the Basic Space Law, passed in 2008. There has not been a definitive resolution to these scholarly debates. Part one tends to focus on the high points of the changes in space policies rather than delving deep into these debates. Furthermore, Japan and the United States have agreed in principle, since 1951, that Japan would gradually assume greater responsibility for its own defense, and as U.S., French, and Australian strategic reviews have noted since 2001, space capabilities have become critical to most countries' modern defense efforts. The same argument can be made, and indeed has been made, for Japan.[273]

Nearly simultaneous to the United States' entry into the ANZUS treaty, the United States and Japan entered into the Security Treaty Between the United States and Japan and the San Francisco Peace Treaty in September 1951. The security treaty included provisions that would limit Japan's re-militarization in the coming years and affect, at least indirectly, Japan's military space activities. As a result of the security treaty, the United States was required to protect Japan militarily, until such time as Japan could "assume responsibility

---

[273] Prime Minister's Office, *National Security Strategy 2013* (provisional translation), December 17, 2013, 19, http://japan.kantei.go.jp/96_abe/documents/2013/__icsFiles/afieldfile/2013/12/17/NSS.pdf.

for its own defense against direct and indirect aggression, [while] always avoiding any armament which could be an offensive threat or serve other than to promote peace and security." [274]

The Treaty of Mutual Cooperation and Security between the United States of America and Japan replaced the Security Treaty between the United States and Japan in 1960. Similar to the ANZUS treaty in the type of response that it required to military aggression but more limited geographically, the Treaty of Mutual Cooperation stated that "each Party recognizes that an armed attack against either Party in the territories under the administration of Japan would be dangerous to its own peace and safety and declares that it would act to the common danger in accordance with its constitutional provisions and processes."[275] What these constitutional provisions mean to the actual practice of collective self-defense is discussed more in part D.

Among its other results, the Treaty of San Francisco ended the immediate postwar prohibitions on rocket research in Japan in 1951.[276] In the mid-1950s, a researcher at Tokyo University named Hideo Itakawa was thus able to begin Japanese research on small solid-fueled rockets for use in launching scientific experiments. Itakawa and his group of researchers formed the nucleus of Japan's Institute of Space and Aeronautical Science, established in 1964. An internationally oriented group of researchers led by Kankuro Kaneshige headed Japanese research on liquid-fueled rockets for use in launching industrially-oriented applications satellites in the 1960s. Kaneshige chaired the National Space Activities Council, which later merged with a division of the Ministry of Posts and Telecommunications to form Japan's National Aeronautics and Space Development Agency (NASDA) in 1969. Although the existence of multiple, non-aligned groups of space researchers in Japan hindered efforts at international collaboration, NASA encouraged Japanese development of liquid-fueled rockets, agreeing to provide Japan with

---

[274] United States Government, *Security TreatybBetween the United States and Japan; September 8, 1951*, September 8, 1951, http://avalon.law.yale.edu/20th_century/japan001.asp#1.

[275] United States Government, *Treaty of Mutual Cooperation and Security between the United States of America and Japan*, January 19, 1960, 3, http://afe.easia.columbia.edu/ps/japan/mutual_cooperation_ treaty.pdf.

[276] Krige, et al., *NASA in the World*, 186-192.

Thor-Delta rocket technology in 1969. This assistance contradicted National Security Action Memorandum 334, introduced in chapter two, but the U.S. government deemed it acceptable due to the perception that Japan needed to provide a symbolic response to Chinese advances in nuclear technology. Japan used an indigenously developed solid-fuel rocket to launch its first orbital satellite from Kagoshima Space Center in early 1970.[277] Japan began launching satellites using a variant of the liquid-fueled Thor-Delta rocket in 1975.

In 1969, Japan's lower house of Parliament passed a resolution stating that Japan could use space only for peaceful, non-military purposes.[278] This law represented a fundamentally different interpretation of the 1967 Outer Space Treaty than that reached by most of the treaty's other signatories, including the United States. This interpretation of the Outer Space Treaty meant that the use of communication and earth-imaging satellites for military purposes was subject to parsimonious debate and scrutiny in Japan until the Diet passed the Basic Space Law in 2008. By interpreting peaceful to mean defensive rather than non-military, the new Basic Space Law permitted the Japan Self-Defense Forces (JSDF) to use satellites militarily with fewer obstacles than ever before.

Collaboration in civil-space endeavors between Japan and the United States grew in the 1970s.[279] NASA agreed to host Japanese scientific experiments in the Space Lab, which U.S. space shuttles housed occasionally on flights. Likewise, Japan agreed to fund the construction of a ground station for Landsat. By the early 1980s, Japan was partnering extensively with NASA on science and technology projects, including in the early planning and development of the Space Station, for which it later built the Japanese Experimental Module.

---

[277] Richard Kruse, "Japanese Launch Vehicles," *Historic Spacecraft*, accessed May 3, 2018, http://historicspacecraft.com/Rockets_Japanese.html.

[278] Manuel Mariquez, "Japan's Space Law Revision: the Next Step toward Re-Militarization?" Nuclear Threat Initiative, January 1, 2008, http://www.nti.org/analysis/articles/japans-space-law-revision/.

[279] Krige, et al., *NASA in the World*, 193-194.

Despite the peaceful purposes resolution then in effect, the Japanese began to ease restrictions regarding the JSDF's use of telecommunications satellites in the 1980s.[280] In 1985, the JSDF purchased terminals to communicate over the U.S. Navy's *Fleet Satellite Communications* system.[281] Japan Defense Agency also began to acquire commercial imagery from the *SPOT* and *Landsat* satellites in the mid-1980s.[282] The Japanese government started to support research into remote-sensing technologies at the same time. This resulted in NASDA developing two *Marine Observation Satellites*.[283] NASDA launched the two satellites on Japanese variants of the American Thor and Delta rockets in 1987 and 1990. The Japanese military went on to employ the *Marine Observation Satellites* to image Chinese construction on disputed territories in the South China Sea in 1993, marking an early example of the Japanese utilizing indigenously developed satellites for military reconnaissance.[284]

The Japan Defense Agency, and other government organizations began to study the possibility of building and launching dedicated reconnaissance satellites in the early 1990s, after the United States brought "Operation Desert Storm" to a successful conclusion.[285] North Korea's launch of missiles into the Sea of Japan in 1993 and over Japanese territory in 1998 provided further impetus for a reconnaissance satellite program. In 2003, Japan launched its first electro-optical and radar reconnaissance satellites, known as the *Information Gathering Satellites (IGS)*.[286] As enumerated in part three, additional *IGS* launches would follow over the coming years.

---

[280] Christopher Hughes, "Japan, Ballistic Missile Defence and remilitarisation," *Space Policy*, April 2, 2013, 131, http://dx.doi.org/10.1016/j.spacepol.2013.03.004.

[281] Maeda Sawako, "Transformation of Japanese Space Policy: From the 'Peaceful Use of space' to the 'Basic Law on Space'," *The Asia-Pacific Journal,* vol. 7, no. 1, November 2, 2009, 2.

[282] William W. Radcliffe, "Origins and Current State of Japan's Reconnaissance Satellite Program (U)," *Studies in Intelligence*, vol. 54, no. 3, September 2010, 10.

[283] Gunter Dirk Krebs, "MOS 1a, 1b (Momo 1a, 1b)," *Gunter's Space Page*, accessed April 27, 2018, http://space.skyrocket.de/doc_sdat/mos.htm.

[284] Radcliffe, "Origins and Current State," 10.

[285] Radcliffe, "Origins and Current State," 9-11.

[286] William Graham, "Japanese H-IIA launches with IGS spy satellite," *NASA Spaceflight.com*, January 31, 2015, https://www.nasaspaceflight.com/2015/01/japanese-h-iia-igs-mission/.

In the early 2000s, the Japanese government consolidated its civil space agencies into the Ministry of Education, Culture, Sports, Science and Technology in 2001, creating the Japan Aerospace Exploration Agency (JAXA) in 2003.[287] This consolidation effectively placed the majority of Japan's space budget under the supervision of an education bureaucrat.[288] A prominent American critic on Japanese space policy, Paul Kallender, estimated nearly a decade later that the Ministry of Education, Culture, Sports, Science and Technology controlled 60 percent of the Japanese government's 3.75 billion U.S. dollar annual space budget through its contributions to JAXA.[289]

Among its other provisions, the 2008 Basic Space Law (mentioned earlier) also contributed to this consolidation of Japanese space activities. It established the Strategic Headquarters for Space Policy, which helped to unify the disparate space interests represented by Cabinet members in several different ministries until that time. In 2012, the Diet passed an additional law to refine the organization of space activities within the Prime Minister's Cabinet Office and established the Office for National Space Policy to inform the decisions of the Strategic Headquarters for Space Policy.[290]

Following passage of the Basic Space Law in 2008, Japan promulgated its first ever Basic Plan on Space Policy in 2009. This was followed by new plans in 2013, 2015, and 2016. The 2015 plan was notable in that it aligned investment decisions for space technology with Japan's first ever National Security Strategy, released in 2013.[291] The 2013 National Security Strategy recognized that Japan needed to make more effective use of satellites "for the operation of the [sic] SDF units, information-gathering and analysis, maritime domain awareness, telecommunications, positioning, navigation, and timing,"

[287] Keiichi Anan, "Administrative reform of the Japanese Space Policy Structures in 2012," *Space Policy*, July 17, 2013, 210, http://dx.doi.org/10.1016/j.spacepol.2013.06.001.

[288] Kazuto Suzuki, "Transforming Japan's space policy-making," *Space Policy*, vol. 23, April 2, 2007, 75, doi: 10.1016/j.spacepol.2007.02.001.

[289] Paul Kallender-Umezu, "A New Direction for Japan's Space Program?" *Aviation Week and Space Technology*, May 6, 2013, 36.

[290] Anan, "Administrative reform," 12.

[291] Office of National Space Policy, "New 'Basic Plan on Space Policy' (Tentative Translation, January 16th, 2015)," January 16, 2015, 1, http://aerospace-wpengine.netdna-ssl.com/wp-content/uploads/2018/04/Japan-Basic-Plan-9Jan15.pdf [translated by Aerospace].

and that it would improve its SSA system.[292] Additionally, the 2015 plan recognized that the United States had modified its approach to space policy, as it had moved from a policy meant to ensure independence and space dominance to one focused on international partnerships and resiliency.[293] The plan noted that the United States had demonstrated this change in focus during a ministerial conference the previous year, in which the United States and Japan had discussed their complementary and mutual interests in PNT systems, space-enabled missile defense, and satellite imagery. The 2015 Basic Plan for Space Policy stated that the Japanese government would take steps to reinforce cooperation with the United States in these mission areas.

Paul Kallender summarized Japan's Basic Plan for Space Policy in 2016. He characterized it as "the first really implementable policy,"[294] which was "designed to support a more proactive US-Japan alliance role in containing China, and robustly defend Japan against North Korean ballistic missile threats."[295] Unlike the previous plans, the fourth Basic Plan on Space Policy was fully funded.[296] Kallender explained that the allocation of resources in the Basic Plan on Space Policy reflected the reorganization of the Cabinet Office that had started in 2008. This reorganization allowed the Cabinet Office to exercise greater control over the individual ministries, especially the Ministry of Education, Culture, Sports, Science and Technology, as the fourth Basic Plan on Space Policy was being developed. The plan supported the U.S.-Japan alliance by applying resources to the whole-of-government space efforts agreed upon in the US-Japan Guidelines for Defense Cooperation, agreed upon in 2015.

The government of Japan committed to expanding its programs in several space mission areas in the fourth Basic Plan on Space Policy. First, the government announced

---

[292] Prime Minister's Office, "National Security Strategy 2013," 19.

[293] Office of National Space Policy, "New 'Basic Plan'," 4-5.

[294] Paul Kallender, "Japan's New Dual-Use Space Policy: The Long Road to the 21st Century," Institut Français des Relations Internationales, November 2016, 3.

[295] Kallender, "Japan's New Dual," 3.

[296] Kallender, "Japan's New Dual," 7-10.

that it would deploy a total of seven Quasi-Zenith Satellite System PNT satellites.[297] Second, it committed JAXA and the newly formed Ministry of Defense to collaborate in creating a functional SSA system by the middle of 2018. Third, the plan marked the government's decision to expand the *IGS* constellation to 10 satellites. Fourth, the plan directed JAXA and the Ministry of Defense to develop an experimental missile-warning satellite. Fifth and last, it tasked JAXA with developing two types of experimental reconnaissance satellites, novel in their size and maneuverability.

Kallender noted that Japan's annual space budget would increase to roughly 5 billion U.S. dollars annually, of which approximately 40 percent would go to defense programs.[298] In late 2017, the Strategic Headquarters for Space Policy issued a revised implementation plan for the fourth Basic Plan on Space Policy. This implementation plan informs the presentation of Japanese military space capabilities in part three of this chapter.

B. HISTORICAL COLLABORATION

The previous section introduced American contributions to Japanese rocketry in the late-1960s and to Japanese SATCOM in the mid-1980s. This section looks at other areas of historical, space-related collaboration and interdependence affecting the defense establishments in Japan and the United States. As a matter of economic policy, the Reagan and Bush administrations pushed for a change in Japanese trade practices during the late 1980s. Using Article 301 of the U.S. Trade Act of 1988, the Bush administration threatened to invoke wide-ranging trade sanctions on the Japanese high-technology industry to stop Japan from protecting its satellite industry specifically.[299] This threat of sanctions and the negotiations that followed resulted in the Japanese government agreeing to permit international bidding on procurement contracts for the country's non-research and development satellites.[300]

---

[297] Kallender, "Japan's New Dual," 11-12.

[298] Kallender, "Japan's New Dual," 13.

[299] James Clayton, "Japan's Aerospace Industry Takes Off," *The Christian Science Monitor*, January 31, 1990.

[300] Suzuki, "Transforming Japan's space," 74.

As it turned out, this trade agreement placed the Japanese government in a dilemma when considering how to characterize and manage the *IGS* program. Based on the trade agreement with the United States, reached in 1990, characterizing *IGS* as a multi-purpose satellite would have opened it up to public bidding; whereas, characterizing it as a defense satellite was precluded by the peaceful purposes resolution passed by the Diet.[301] The solution to the dilemma was to place the *IGS* program under the Cabinet Secretariat. Over the coming years, this placement decision would expose shortcomings in the management structure for Japanese space activities, which contributed to early failures in the *IGS* program. In turn, these failures led to calls for reform, which the Diet incorporated into the Basic Law for Space Policy less than three years later.

The remainder of part two discusses recent military space collaboration between Japan and the United States in specific mission areas. This includes collaboration in missile warning, PNT, and, most recently, SSA. Similar to the way it had constrained Japan's satellite reconnaissance program, Japanese law placed an uncommon restraint on the country's options for ballistic missile defense. In 2007, Kazuto Sazuki wrote: "The Japanese government has taken a unique interpretation of its Constitution Article 9, namely that Japan holds the right to collective defense, but will not exercise it. If an enemy missile is set and ready for operation, the country would not be able to launch a counter attack missile unless the command comes from a Japanese early warning satellite."[302] Nevertheless, the Japanese government followed through on its agreement to acquire ballistic missile defense systems from the United States in 2003.[303] These systems consisted of the Patriot Advance Capability-3 and Standard Missile 3 Block 2A by 2010. Additionally, the U.S. Army established a Joint Tactical Ground System unit and an associated facility in Misawa, Japan in 2007 and 2008, respectively.[304] Recent upgrades to the Joint Tactical Ground System have allowed it to directly downlink data from both *DSP*

---

[301] Suzuki, "Transforming Japan's space," 76-77.

[302] Suzuki, "Transforming Japan's space," 77.

[303] Hughes, "Japan, Ballistic Missile," 129.

[304] Allison Day, "Joint Tactical Ground Station Opens at Misawa," Pacific Air Forces, January 23, 2008, http://www.pacaf.af.mil/News/Article-Display/Article/596548/joint-tactical-ground-station-opens-at-misawa/.

and *SBIRS* satellites to warn and potentially cue supported forces in the event of a ballistic missile launch.[305]

In 2011, Japan's first Quasi-Zenith Satellite System PNT satellite entered into operation.[306] Two of the Quasi-Zenith ground stations were located on U.S. islands in the Pacific Ocean, on Hawaii and Guam. Japan's National Space Policy Secretariat announced in March 2018 that Quasi-Zenith Satellite System services would begin operations by the end of the year.[307] The system promises to improve PNT services to Japan beyond what GPS satellites provide to it currently, given Japan's mountainous geography and built-up urban environments.[308]

In 2013, Japan and the United States began discussions and official dialogues regarding SSA data sharing.[309] In May 2013, Japan and the United States signed a memorandum of understanding as a result of which U.S. Strategic Command and NASA began to provide SSA data to Japan.[310] In May 2014, the two countries reached an agreement for JAXA to provide SSA data to the United States. Despite this progress and the participation of the Department of Defense in the SSA framework, the four Comprehensive Dialogues on Space between Japan and the United States have been largely civilian affairs. Only in the joint press release from the fourth Comprehensive Dialogues on Space, in 2017, was the participation of the Japan Ministry of Defense and the U.S. Department of Defense in the talks explicitly acknowledged.[311] As the Ministry of

---

[305] United States Army, "MDSS Project Office," accessed April 28, 2018, https://www.msl.army.mil/Pages/mdss/jtags.html.

[306] GPS.gov, "Joint Announcement on Japan-United States GPS Cooperation," July 24, 2013, https://www.gps.gov/policy/cooperation/japan/2013-joint-announcement/.

[307] National Space Policy Secretariat, "Quasi-Zenith Satellite System," March 11, 2018, https://web.archive.org/web/20180311021244/http://qzss.go.jp/en/overview/notices/service_180302.html.

[308] National Space Policy Secretariat, "[Movie] Quasi-Zenith Satellite System 'QZSS'," December 3, 2016, http://qzss.go.jp/en/overview/downloads/movie_qzss.html.

[309] Peter B. de Selding, "U.S., Japan Pledge Closer Cooperation on Space Surveillance," *Space News*, October 4, 2013, http://spacenews.com/37551us-japan-pledge-closer-cooperation-on-space-surveillance/.

[310] Shizuo Yamamoto, "Overview of JAXA Activities on Sustainable Space Development and Space Situational Awareness," JAXA, February 26, 2015, 12, http://www.jsforum.or.jp/debrisympo/2015/pdf/09S2DS2A2015_JAXA_KNote_0225.pdf.

[311] U.S. Department of State, "Joint Statement: The Fourth Meeting of the U.S.-Japan Comprehensive Dialogue on Space," May 17, 2017, https://www.state.gov/r/pa/prs/ps/2017/05/270946.htm.

Defense's SSA network comes online in 2018 and beyond, the Japanese government plans to develop guidelines to further its cooperation with the United States, to include sending JSDF personnel to work at U.S. Strategic Command.[312]

C.   CURRENT MILITARY SPACE ORGANIZATION AND CAPABILITIES

The focus of this section is Japanese organization and capabilities for military space. Japan possesses or will soon possess similar military space capabilities to France. Therefore, this section is organized similar to the that earlier section, beginning with space-based imagery, then proceeding to missile warning, PNT, weather, and space launch.

According to William Radcliffe, Japan merged "the 'Central Geography Unit' of the [Ground Self-Defense Force] with the satellite imagery divisions of the other [JSDF] branches" to form Defense Intelligence Headquarters Imagery Directorate in 1997.[313] The Imagery Directorate primarily exploited commercial imagery purchased from U.S. companies during its first few years of existence.[314] By 2004, the Imagery Directorate's resources had grown, however, and it was renamed the Directorate for Geospatial Intelligence. At that time, the directorate employed 321 civilian and uniformed analysts.[315] These analysts specialized in three-dimensional mapping and in analyzing satellite imagery.[316]

The Prime Minister's Cabinet Satellite Intelligence Center is responsible for the *IGS* optical and radar imaging satellites.[317] The current *IGS* constellation has three optical and four radar satellites. The satellites reportedly have .6 m and 1 m resolution,

---

[312] National Space Policy Secretariat, "Implementation Plan of the Basic Plan on Space Policy," December 17, 2017, 46, http://www8.cao.go.jp/space/english/basicplan/2017/basicplan.pdf.

[313] Radcliffe, "Origins and Current State," 12.

[314] Radcliffe, "Origins and Current State," 18.

[315] Radcliffe, "Origins and Current State," 18.

[316] Radcliffe, "Origins and Current State," 18.

[317] William Graham, "Japanese H-IIA launches IGS Optical 6 satellite," *NASA Spaceflight.com*, February 26, 2018, https://www.nasaspaceflight.com/2018/02/japanese-h-iia-rocket-igs-6-launch/.

respectively. One tracking website estimates that the *IGS* are employed in 93-98 degree inclinations at roughly 500 km altitude.[318]

Two *IGS* are currently in development with projected launch dates in 2019 and 2023.[319] JAXA is building a data-relay satellite to support the growing number of *IGS* used to gather imagery.[320] It is scheduled, too, to launch in 2019.[321] Over the next decade, Japan will move toward a total of 10 satellites in the *IGS* constellation, composed of four core *IGS* satellites, four satellites currently referred to as *Surveillance Capability Augmentation Satellites*, and two data-relay satellites.

Ground stations at Tomakomai, Akune, and Kitaura, Japan support *IGS* operations.[322] A fourth *IGS* ground station is located near Perth, Australia. The main control and analysis center is located in Tokyo on the north side of the Defense Ministry headquarters. This facility is referred to as the Cabinet Satellite Intelligence Center, and it falls under the Cabinet Intelligence and Research Office.

The first director of the Cabinet Satellite Intelligence Center was a retired general.[323] Furthermore, approximately 10 percent of personnel working at the center in 2001 were from the JSDF. Up to 300 people may now work at the Cabinet Satellite Intelligence Center.[324] An additional 80 personnel are likely needed to operate the four *IGS* ground stations, bringing the total number of personnel directly associated with *IGS* operations up to 380.[325]

---

[318] NY2O.com, "Military Satellites," accessed April 27, 2018, http://www.n2yo.com/satellites/?c=30 &srt=1&dir=1.

[319] National Space Policy Secretariat, "Implementation Plan," 11.

[320] National Space Policy Secretariat, "Implementation Plan," 11.

[321] Kallender, "Japan's New Dual," 11.

[322] Radcliffe, "Origins and Current State," 17-18.

[323] Radcliffe, "Origins and Current State," 17.

[324] Radcliffe, "Origins and Current State," 17.

[325] Radcliffe, "Origins and Current State," 17-18.

The Japanese government has long considered developing a space-based infrared sensor for missile early warning.[326] Moreover, in 2014, a Japanese lawmaker and former chairman of the Space Policy Committee, Hiroshi Imazu, expressed a personal interest in the U.S. Navy's Slow Walker program. As part of the Slow Walker program, the U.S. Navy used *DSP* satellites data to track the movements of Soviet bombers in the 1980s.[327] In fiscal year 2020, JAXA is projected to host a prototype dual-wavelength infrared sensor on its *Advanced Land Observing Satellite 3* in a cooperative arrangement with the Ministry of Defense.[328] This cooperative arrangement suggests that *Advanced Land Observing Satellite 3* may, itself, be employed as a dual-use satellite. JAXA states that *Advanced Land Observing Satellite 3* will operate in three modes, provide panchromatic imagery at up to .8 m resolution and multispectral imagery in six bands at up to 3.2 m resolution, and have a pointing capability of up to 60 degrees in all directions.[329]

In his analysis of the Basic Plan for Space Policy, in 2016, Kallender suggests that Japan was also considering whether to develop satellites to gather signals intelligence.[330] However, the 2017 implementation plan makes no mention of a signals intelligence satellite, nor does signals intelligence figure into cooperative agreements with the United States, such as the Guidelines for Japan-U.S. Defense Cooperation.

For SATCOM, Japan's defense forces currently rely upon a combination of *Superbird* and *DSN* satellites.[331] The two *Superbird* satellites are owned and operated by SKY Perfect JSAT Corporation. The Ministry of Defense projects to stop using the *Superbird-D* satellite by the end of 2018. It plans to use *Superbird C-2* through 2020.

[326] Paul Kallender-Umezu, "Profile | Hiroshi Imazu, former Chairman, Space Policy Committee, Liberal Democratic Party of Japan," *Space News*, October 27, 2014, spacenews.com/42331profile-hiroshi-imazu-former-chairman-space-policy-committee-liberal/.

[327] Dwayne A. Day, "Ugly little gem: The Teal Ruby satellite," *The Space Review*, September 14 2015, http://www.thespacereview.com/article/2599/2.

[328] National Space Policy Secretariat, "Implementation Plan," 84.

[329] JAXA, "Advanced Optical Satellite (ALOS-3)," accessed May 5, 2018, http://global.jaxa.jp/projects/sat/alos3/.

[330] Kallender, "Japan's New Dual," 13.

[331] National Space Policy Secretariat, "Implementation Plan," 33.

Superbird C-2 is located at 144 east longitude and permits SHF communications.[332] In 2013, the Ministry of Defense contracted DSN Corporation to build and operate two SHF satellites.[333] *DSN-1* is a hosted payload on *Superbird-8*. *Superbird-8* is a commercial satellite located at 162 degrees east longitude.[334] It began operations in 2018 after a two-year launch delay. *DSN-2* is a dedicated military satellite.[335] It is located at 92 degrees east longitude, over the Indian Ocean, and began operations in 2017.[336]

As mentioned in the previous section, Japan developed the Quasi-Zenith Satellite System to improve its access to PNT. The Quasi-Zenith Satellite System places all four of its satellites in a highly-inclined geosynchronous orbit centered at 136 degrees east longitude.[337] Each satellite achieves its maximum dwell time at 42 degrees north latitude to maximize coverage over Japan, before speeding through its orbit over the southern hemisphere. The system's signals are fully compatible with GPS and require no changes to existing GPS receivers. The Quasi-Zenith Satellite System constellation will incorporate three additional satellites in fiscal year 2023, when it is scheduled to begin operations as a seven satellite constellation.[338] This will ensure that four of the constellation's seven satellites are located nearly over Japan's mainland at any one time.

Japan currently employs two geostationary meteorological satellites: *Himawari-8* is the primary, and *Himawari-9* operates in standby.[339] They are positioned at 140.7 degrees east longitude.[340] The Japan Meteorological Agency operates the *Himawari*

---

[332] SKY Perfect JSAT, "Superbird-C2," accessed May 12, 2018, http://www.jsat.net/en/contour/superbird-c2.html.

[333] Spaceflight 101.com, "DSN-2 Satellite," accessed May 12, 2018, https://spaceflight101.com/h-iia-dsn-2/dsn-2/.

[334] Gunter Dirk Krebs, "DSN 1 / Superbird 8 (Kirameki 1 / Superbird B3)," *Gunter's Space Page*, accessed May 12, 2018, http://space.skyrocket.de/doc_sdat/dsn-1_superbird-8.htm.

[335] Spaceflight 101.com, "DSN-2 Satellite."

[336] NY2O.com, "DSN-2," accessed May 12, 2018, https://www.n2yo.com/?s=41940&live=1.

[337] Space Flight 101, "Quasi-Zenith Satellite System," accessed May 6, 2018, http://spaceflight101.com/spacecraft/qzss/.

[338] National Space Policy Secretariat, "Implementation Plan," 5.

[339] National Space Policy Secretariat, "Implementation Plan," 20.

[340] Japan Meteorological Agency, "Meteorological Satellites -Japan Meteorological Agency (JMA)-," accessed May 6, 2018, http://www.jma.go.jp/jma/jma-eng/satellite/.

satellites and works in partnership with EUMETSAT and the National Oceanic and Atmospheric Administration to provide worldwide satellite weather coverage.[341]

JAXA is the primary Japanese agency responsible for providing SSA data. It employs the JAXA Satellite Tracking Station Network and the Bisei and Kamisaibara Space Guard centers to this end.[342] The JAXA Satellite Tracking Station Network includes four domestic and four international tracking and control stations.[343] The international stations are located at Christmas Island; Santiago, Chile; Perth, Australia; and Gran Canaria Island, located off the coast of West Africa. The optical sensor at Bisei Space Guard Center is capable of monitoring objects a small as .8 m in diameter, located from 68 degrees east to 200 degrees east along the geostationary belt.[344] The radar sensor at Kamisaibara Space Guard Center can track up to 10 objects simultaneously and is capable of tracking objects 1 m in diameter from a range of 600 km. According to JAXA's SSA system project manager, Mayumi Matsuura, Japan plans to develop capabilities enabling JAXA to monitor objects .1 m in diameter in the coming years.[345]

Japan currently has three separate satellite launch vehicles, with a fourth under development.[346] Epsilon is a small, solid-fueled rocket. It can launch up to a 450 kg payload into a 500 km circular orbit, in one of two optional configurations. H-IIB is a two-stage liquid-fueled rocket. Its primary purpose is to launch the H-II Transfer Vehicle to the International Space Station. The H-IIA is Japan's mainstay heavy launch vehicle. It is operated by Mitsubishi Heavy Industries with oversight from JAXA. It can launch up to a 4 metric ton payload into a geosynchronous transfer orbit. The H3 launch vehicle is under

---

[341] National Oceanic and Atmospheric Administration, "International Partners in the Sky: Satellite Partnerships," February 12, 2018, https://www.nesdis.noaa.gov/content/international-partners-sky-satellite-partnerships.

[342] Yamamoto, "Overview of JAXA," 5.

[343] JAXA, "Overview of the Tracking and Control Center at the Tsukuba Space Center," accessed May 12, 2018, 3, http://www.jaxa.jp/countdown/f11/presskit/kiku8_tracking_e.pdf.

[344] Yamamoto, "Overview of JAXA," 6-7.

[345] Mayumi Matsuura, in "Preventing Collisions between Debris and Spacecraft" by Doug Messier, *Parabolic Arc*, May 9, 2017, http://www.parabolicarc.com/2017/05/09/preventing-collisions-between-debris-spacecraft/.

[346] JAXA, "Space Transportation Systems," accessed May 6, 2018, http://global.jaxa.jp/projects/rockets/.

development, with its maiden flight planned for fiscal year 2020. The H3 launch capacity will exceed that of the H-II rockets. Japan aims to capture a share of the commercial space launch market with it.

Japan has two space launch facilities: Tanegashima and Uchinoura, also known as Kagoshima. Both facilities are located at 31 degrees north latitude.[347][348]

D. ANALYSIS

As before, part four analyzes the information uncovered in the first three parts to identify areas for potential military space collaboration between Japan and the United States. Based on the material presented in part one, Japan has successfully consolidated its space leadership under the Headquarters for Space Policy in the last few years. Combined with the emergence of a national security strategy that recognizes the importance of space to Japan's defense, this has led significant increases in spending on Japan's military space capabilities. With a budget for military space now amounting to approximately 2 billion U.S. dollars per year, Japan is expending about three times as much on military space capabilities as France is spending on it currently.

Despite Japan's expanding capabilities and its expressed desire to further its space-related defense cooperation with the United States, collaboration in space between each country's military establishments has still been modest. A significant barrier to effective collaboration in this domain was touched upon in part B: the idea that Article 9 of Japan's constitution precluded Japan from exercising collective self-defense. Nevertheless, a cabinet decision in 2014 established that Japan did indeed have the right to come to the aid of a close ally under attack once specific conditions had been met. While this decision did not go as far as the Abe government would have liked, it led to a revision of the Guidelines for Japan-U.S. Defense Cooperation in 2015.[349] In a likely reference to the space and cyber

---

[347] Elizabeth Howell, "Tanegashima: Japan's Largest Space Center," *Space.com*, September 30, 2016, https://www.space.com/34270-tanegashima-space-center.html.

[348] Astronautix, "Kagoshima," accessed May 6, 2018, http://www.astronautix.com/k/kagoshima.html.

[349] Adam P. Liff, "Policy by Other Means: Collective Self-Defense and the Politics of Japan's Postwar Constitutional Reinterpretations," *Asia Policy*, no. 24, July 2017, 140, https://doi.org/10.1353/asp.2017.0035.

domains, the guidelines indicated that Japan and the United States would respond to non-geographic threats "that will have an important influence on Japan's peace and security."[350] This announcement portended greater collaboration in space, as did a statement made in Japan's national security strategy regarding the Ministry of Defense increasing its focus on counter-intelligence. According to the statement, Japan would expand its efforts to protect "Specially Designated Secrets."[351] Increased defense-related space collaboration with the United States would tend to result in the accumulation of a few more secrets such as these.

Based on part C, Japan has a not-insignificant capability to image from space and has developed its ability to analyze satellite images for over 20 years. This capability would and should provide an intelligence windfall for the United States. Moreover, Japan appears to be setting itself apart from the United States' other allies in space in working to develop a space-based infrared capability. Tying into these infrared sensors would help to improve the United States theater missile defense. Furthermore, as evidenced by the Quasi-Zenith Satellite System, which maximizes PNT availability over the Japanese mainland, Japanese satellite systems are likely to be regionally optimized, presenting the United States with the opportunity to tie-in to these systems while maintaining a more globally optimized capability itself.

The United States already benefits from weather data provided by Japan's meteorological satellites. Ideally, the Department of Defense would be able to use the space launch facilities to launch national payloads in the event of an emergency, as a means of providing assured access to space.

Japan's ability to conduct SSA appears to nearly match France's ability. However, Japan is working to develop a more integrated SSA network than it has currently, one which the JSDF can better utilize. As the JSDF gains more control over and access to Japan's SSA network, it will be interesting to see how SSA agreements with the United States develop. In 2017, Japan participated in the "Global Sentinel" table-top exercise led by

---

[350] Ministry of Defense, "The Guidelines for Japan-U.S. Defense Cooperation," April 27, 2015, 7, http://www.mod.go.jp/e/d_act/anpo/shishin_20150427e.html.

[351] Prime Minister's Office, "National Security Strategy 2013," 18.

U.S. Strategic Command.[352] The United States' five-eye partners, as well as France, Germany, Spain, Italy, and the Republic of Korea also participated.[353] Given the partners included in the exercise, the exercise may have well involved the sharing of classified SSA data. Nevertheless, the United States does not appear to have reached a long-term agreement to share classified SSA data with Japan, as it earlier did with Australia and France. Establishing an agreement to share classified SSA data with Japan appears to be one of the next logical steps for the United States to take to strengthen its military cooperation with Japan.

---

[352] S., *Fiscal Year 2019*, 12.

[353] S., *Fiscal Year 2019*, 12.

THIS PAGE INTENTIONALLY LEFT BLANK

V.   SUMMARY AND CONCLUSION

Beginning in the early 1990s, countries around the world could observe that the United States used space systems to significantly increase the combat effectiveness of its military forces.   Potential adversaries, such as China, took note and began to develop strategies and means to jeopardize space assets.   The U.S. Congress responded to the increased threat to our valued space systems by commissioning a study in the 1999 National Defense Authorization Act. Released in 2001, the study set the United States on a path toward a National Security Space Strategy.   The United States released its first-ever National Security Space Strategy in 2011.   The strategy prescribed increased partnering with U.S. allies in response to a contested space environment.   Space policy leaders in the United States argued that allied partnering in space would help to ensure that the U.S. military's space capabilities were resilient to attack, and that this resiliency would deter attacks on our space assets in the first place.   Although some scholars began to challenge the success of the 2011 National Security Space Strategy in creating a framework that deterred aggressive action in space in later years, the question of whether the strategy was effectively fostering allied collaboration in space was largely absent from their critiques. As a result, this thesis set out to determine the mission areas in which the United States was partnering with its military allies in space and how the United States might benefit from operating as a coalition space force.

A.   CASE STUDIES

This thesis took a case study approach to answer the central research question, examining the evolution, efforts at collaboration, and military space capabilities of three of the United States' closest spacefaring allies: France, Australia, and Japan. One of the most remarkable findings of this analysis was how similar the paths of these three countries had been relative to one another in the military space domain from 2008 onward. France and Australia explicitly recognized the importance of space operations to their military operations in the national defense strategies that they released in the 2008-2009 timeframe. In 2008, Japan signaled the growing importance of space to its military as well by revising its Basic Space Law. In the period following the global financial crisis in 2009, however, each country failed to follow through on its proposed investments in military space systems in the way that it had envisioned just a few years prior. But these failures, ironically, helped to bring organizational reforms to fruition in each country at about the same time. These reforms moved Australia ever closer to a national space agency; whereas France developed a military space command; and Japan developed a space policy headquarters in the Cabinet Office. Moreover, by 2016, each of the countries had developed mechanisms to ensure that its planned investments in military space capabilities were fully funded. Thus, by the end of 2017, all three countries were largely developing the military space capabilities that they had envisioned a decade prior.

This chapter revisits the findings of the case studies, focusing on the mission areas where collaboration between the United States and one of more of the countries has occurred. It briefly discusses the collaboration's motivations and the benefits to help answer the question, "How might the United States benefit from coalition operations in space?" The author then analyzes the Department of Defense's International Space Cooperation Strategy (ISCS) to compare the ends and means of collaboration that it prescribes with the findings from the case studies. Released to the public in May 2017, the Department of Defense ISCS flows from the 2011 National Security Space Strategy but reflects more recent thinking on the subject of space cooperation in the Department of Defense. The chapter and the overall thesis conclude with suggestions for future research.

1.   SSA

The Department of Defense's success in signing SSA-sharing agreements with as many governments as it did over the past eight years may represent its crowning achievement in space cooperation. By November 2017, U.S. Strategic Command had succeeded in signing SSA-sharing agreements with a total of 17 countries.[354] The timing of these agreements was a significant aspect of their success: at the same time that the

---

[354] Wilson Brissett, "US Allies on the Move in Space," *Air Force Magazine*, October 27, 2017, http://www.airforcemag.com/Features/Pages/2017/October%202017/US-Allies-on-the-Move-in-Space.aspx.

space domain was growing in importance in the minds of the military leaders in each of these 17 countries, the Department of Defense found common cause with these leaders and the countries they represented. The title of a Space News article covering events from the 34th Space Symposium captures a critical result of these SSA-sharing agreements, explaining "International SSA agreements could pave the way for further space cooperation."[355] The case of France provides a quintessential example of how this increase in cooperation can occur, as France moved from a basic SSA-sharing agreement, to an advanced agreement, and then to combined space operations with the United States. In addition to building relationships, the SSA-agreements have proliferated the space surveillance sensors that the Department of Defense receives data from globally. Over the last several years, U.S. Strategic Command has leveraged its commercial relationships with Lockheed Martin to lead the "Global Sentinel" exercise, which plans for the operational use of a combined, global SSA network among the United States and several of its allies.[356]

2.   SATCOM

Although space surveillance may be the most talked-about means of collaboration, SATCOM represents one of the most enduring means. SATCOM helps to satisfy a fundamental military requirement to "shoot, move, and communicate," by providing communications well removed from any ground-based infrastructure. As a result of this functionality, NATO has well-established specifications for member states to build their military telecommunications satellites to. Similarly, Japan purchased terminals to link to U.S. military SATCOM before it started using any other military satellite capability.

The United States now has several international partners in the *WGS* program.[357] Geostationary SATCOM is typically the most cost-effective means of acquiring

---

[355] Debra Werner, "International SSA Agreements Could Pave the Way for Further Space Cooperation, Panelists Said," *Space News*, April 18, 2018, http://spacenews.com/international-ssa-agreements-could-pave-the-way-for-further-space-cooperation-panelists-said/.

[356] U.S. Strategic Command Public Affairs, "USSTRATCOM Hosts Space Exercise with International Partners," October 3, 2016, http://www.stratcom.mil/Media/News/News-Article-View/Article/984307/usstratcom-hosts-space-exercise-with-international-partners/.

[357] Arielle Vasquez, "WGS-9 satellite launches from Florida," U.S. Air Force, March 29, 2017, http://www.schriever.af.mil/News/Article-Display/Article/1134074/wgs-9-satellite-launches-from-florida/.

bandwidth, but the bandwidth is decidedly localized. By reaching an agreement for Australia to provide the funds for *WGS-6*, Australia and United States resolved this conundrum in a way that was amenable to both parties. Australia gained worldwide access to SHF communications at the cost of a single geostationary satellite, while the United States got more SHF bandwidth and a more resilient constellation than it would have otherwise. Australia was recently waiting on the United States to conduct an analysis of alternatives of its future SATCOM architecture before making its own acquisitions decisions.

3.   Intelligence, Surveillance, and Reconnaissance

The Department of Defense may still owe a debt of gratitude to the U.S. Geological Survey and NASA for their role in the development of *Landsat-1* and the sharing of Landsat images in the 1960s and 1970s. France got its start at imagery analysis using Landsat images, before developing and exploiting its own dual-use *SPOT* satellites. Prior to developing *IGS*, Japan analyzed images from Landsat and *SPOT* satellites. In the early 1990s, the Department of Defense acquired Eagle Vision to download *SPOT* images, and it has been using and distributing commercial imagery to friendly foreign military forces ever since.

Australia now acquires its satellite imagery from a U.S. commercial company, images which it can analyze and provide back to the U.S. military as it desires. In this regard, the United States may stand to gain more from the expertise and focus of the imagery analysts in countries such as France, Australia, and Japan than it does from the actual number of raw images that these countries' satellites can provide. It helps if this analysis is in English, of course.

4.   PNT

Australia, France, and Japan have all worked on developing PNT systems, with the work of each country benefiting the U.S. military in some form. Australia assisted the United States in testing of the GPS program, providing both manpower and a location in the southern hemisphere to conduct tests from. France contributed to the development of an independent European PNT capability, which provides a redundant capability to GPS.

Japan developed a regionally-focused PNT system that is fully compatible with GPS. Japan's system will begin operations as a 4-satellite constellation later in 2018. While none of this work will ensure PNT availability in the event of intentional jamming, each country's contributions provides a modicum of benefit to the Department of Defense.

5.   Missile Warning and Defense

Australia has participated in the U.S. missile defense network for over 50 years. Along with the agreements on communications intelligence, the existence of joint U.S.-Australian space research facilities in Australia has contributed significantly to Australia's overall security relationship with the United States. This close relationship has not always been a good thing, as Australian is only now beginning to devote two percent of its GDP to defense expenditures. Nevertheless, recent Australian investments in the Mission Processor to download *SBIRS* data make it a more capable ally in terms of traditional military operations, since this information can contribute to the sound tactical employment of Australian forces. Furthermore, Australia has practiced integrating missile-warning data provided by the United States into its missile defense network since the 1990s. Unlike Australia, Japan is investing in an independent missile-warning satellite system. This capability could also benefit U.S. forces deployed in the region, either through tactical integration or by simply contributing to their security.

6.   Weather

None of militaries in these case studies appeared to exercise direct control over weather satellites. However, U.S. forces have still benefited from weather data that the Japan Meteorological Agency and EUMETSAT satellites provide. Moreover, as a result of its working relationship with EUMETSAT, the U.S. Air Force deferred investment in a meteorological satellite that would have provided weather data over the Indian Ocean. Unfortunately, the situation ended on a sour note when EUMETSAT decided not to replace the satellite that the Air Force was using at the end of its design life.

7. Space Launch

The United States provided Japan with technology that helped it to develop a heavy-lift satellite launch capability despite U.S. policy barring international assistance in this mission area. The United States pursued collaboration in this area to promote Japanese prestige, thereby contributing to the strategic messaging of a U.S. ally.

B. DEPARTMENT OF DEFENSE ISCS

This section analyzes the Department of Defense ISCS in terms of ends, ways, and means; it then discusses the relevance of this thesis' findings to the implementation plan that the ISCS directs. The Department of Defense ISCS clearly establishes mission assurance as one end of international space cooperation.[358] Four more ends are also buried within the first several pages of the document: overcoming constrained resources or promoting sustainability; operating more efficiently and effectively in a coalition environment; assured access; and promoting U.S. national security interests. The single overarching way in which the U.S. Department of Defense will achieve international space cooperation is through multi-domain interoperability. The document prescribes advancing this interoperability in six different areas: legal, policy, doctrinal, and operational principles; technology research and development; acquisition and production; technology and information sharing; techniques, tactics, and procedures relating to space operations; and education, training, and exchanges of personnel. The means associated with these ends are partners' and allies' space-related capabilities.

This thesis has shown that the United States has employed the strategy set forth in the current Department of Defense ISCS in the past. This knowledge should inspire confidence in the Department of Defense components that its international partners and allies possess the necessary political leadership, milestones, capabilities, and trust in handling sensitive information for the components to develop realistic and achievable implementation plans that can contribute to the United States' overall deterrence strategy.

---

[358] Office of the Assistant Secretary of Defense for Homeland Defense, *Department of Defense International Space Cooperation Strategy*, January 1, 2017, 1-3, http://www.dtic.mil/dtic/tr/fulltext/u2/1034871.pdf.

Furthermore, there appears to be room for growth in international space cooperation in the immediate future in regards to doctrine and organization, know-how, capabilities, and trust, with attendant benefits to U.S. security.

C.   SUGGESTIONS FOR FUTURE RESEARCH

At the doctrinal and organizational level, the components of the Department of Defense are currently fleshing out their concepts for multi-domain battle. This can be seen in the recent development of the Multi-Domain Battle concept in the Army and the establishment of the Deputy Commandant for Information and Marine Expeditionary Force Information Groups in the Marine Corps, among other initiatives across the services. Similarly, space control doctrine is actively being refined, although the National Space Defense Center has yet to achieve its full manning levels. Our international partners can be integral to these developments or, as is occurring mostly, they can be integrated into it after the fact. Either way, the Department of Defense ISCS envisions incorporating allied and partner capabilities into doctrine and organizations that do not yet fully exist. As these rapidly developing doctrines and organizations take shape, so too can the relationship of our international partners to them.

With regard to know-how, little evidence was uncovered in the case studies of our international allies being incorporated into our training and educational institutions to learn about space. One reason for this may be that space education poses security challenges less inherent to other areas of study. For example, policy at the Naval Postgraduate School dictates that international students not be given access to any confidential information, including information that is classified as "For Official Use Only." Nevertheless, the Department of Defense ISCS seemingly envisions cooperation with our trusted partners and allies at much higher security levels than that. Revisiting security policy at Department of Defense training and educational institutions may make the courses of instruction more inviting to our international partners and allies with whom we desire further cooperation in space.

France and Japan are developing new Intelligence, Surveillance, and Reconnaissance capabilities not previously possessed by our allies. Some thought should be given to how to these new systems can complement our existing and planned ELINT and missile-warning architectures.

In regard to launch capability, the National Space Transportation Policy permits U.S. government payloads to be launched on space vehicles manufactured outside the United States by exception.[359] The policy also permits the U.S. government to launch foreign-manufactured vehicles and technology on a case-by-case basis. The processes for launching a close ally's defense satellite from a U.S. government site as well as for launching a U.S. defense asset from an appropriately secure foreign site could be better understood by all parties involved and streamlined. This would help to ensure assured access to space for both the United States and its spacefaring allies.

Finally, the Fiscal Year 2019 National Defense Authorization Act is anticipated to direct the Department of Commerce rather than the Department of Defense to assume responsibility for providing SSA services to foreign governments by 2024.[360] The SSA-sharing agreements that the Department of Defense has signed with 17 countries since 2010 have helped it to establish a common ground with these countries' militaries from which to work toward coalition space operations. With the Department of Commerce assuming some of the Department of Defense's present responsibility for engaging with foreign governments, the Department of Defense would do well to consider how to make the most out of the authority that it currently possesses. This forethought will help to ensure that it continues to engage with new partners and build mutual levels of trust and interoperability with existing ones as this change takes place.

D. CONCLUSION

This thesis has analyzed and further developed the notion that the Department of Defense has to continue to work to collaborate successfully with its spacefaring friends and

---

[359] Office of the President of the United States, *National Space Transportation Policy*, November 21, 2013, 8, https://obamawhitehouse.archives.gov/sites/default/files/microsites/ostp/national_space_transportation_poli cy_11212013.pdf.

[360] Sandra Erwin, "Defense Department Turning over Space Traffic Management to Commerce, but Details still Unclear," *Space News*, May 7, 2018, http://spacenews.com/defense-department-turning-over-space-traffic-management-to-commerce-but-details-still-unclear/.

allies. Fortunately, the Department of Defense has proven its ability to collaborate successfully in space-related endeavors in the past, as this thesis has shown. Compared to the past, however, international recognition that space systems have become critical to military operational effectiveness has grown in recent years. This realization has increased international demand for a variety of space and space-related capabilities and increased the likelihood that future military conflict will extend into space as well. In light of these changes to the operating environment, the Department of Defense has begun pursuing even greater interoperability in space with our friends and allies to make the most out of each country's scarce resources and increase their awareness of the space environment. To the extent that the Department of Defense achieves this interoperability while maintaining an appropriate level of operational security, it will provide the United States with an asymmetric military advantage over its near-peer competitors, Russia and China, for whom such collaboration appears highly unlikely.[361]

---

[361] Moltz, "Coalitions in Space," 16.

THIS PAGE INTENTIONALLY LEFT BLANK

LIST OF REFERENCES

Abbey, Elizabeth. "Australian Defence Signs $100 Million Deal for High-res Satellite Imagery." Spatial Source. August 22, 2017. https://www.spatialsource.com.au/remote-sensing/australian-defense-signs-100-million-deal-high-res-satellite-imagery.

Abbot, Jaimie. "First Space Operations Unit." *Air Force*, vol. 57, no. 9. May 21, 2015. http://www.defence.gov.au/Publications/NewsPapers/Raaf/editions/5709a/5709a.pdf.

Aerospace Technology. "US and Australia Sign Space Situational Awareness Data Sharing Agreement." April 24, 2013. https://www.aerospace-technology.com/uncategorised/newsus-and-australia-sign-space-situational-awareness-data-sharing-agreement/.

Agence France Presse. "Philippe Announces an Unprecedented Increase in the Defense Budget." *Le Figaro*. August 9, 2017. http://www.lefigaro.fr/conjoncture/2017/09/08/20002-20170908ARTFIG00082-philippe-annonce-une-hausse-sans-precedent-du-budget-de-la-defense.php [translated by the author].

Air Power Development Centre. "Evolution of Australian Military Space." Pathfinder: Air Power Development Bulletin iss. 105. February 2009.

Aishwarya, Srivari. "Australia's CASG Deliver Battle-space Awareness Capability to RAAF." *Air Force Technology*. August 25, 2016. https://www.airforce-technology.com/uncategorised/newsaustralias-casg-delivers-battle-space-awareness-capability-to-raaf-4989342/.

Anan, Keiichi. "Administrative Reform of the Japanese Space Policy Structures in 2012." *Space Policy*. July 17, 2013. http://dx.doi.org/10.1016/j.spacepol.2013.06.001.

Asia-Pacific Defence Reporter. "JP 2008 – Heading for the Projects of Concern List." April 2, 2014. https:// www.asiapacificdefencereporter.com/articles/431/JP-2008-heading-for-the-Projects-of-Concern-list.

Astronautix. "Kagoshima." Accessed May 6, 2018. http://www.astronautix.com/k/kagoshima.html.

Australian Aviation. "Boeing, CSIRO Announce New Space Partnership." January 29, 2018. australianaviation.com.au/2018/01/boeing-csiro-announce-new-space-partnership/.

Australia Broadcasting Corporation, "Fact check: Does ANZUS Commit the U.S. to Come to Australia's aid?" ABC News. July 22, 2014, http://www.abc.net.au/news/2014 -07-08/does-anzus-commit-us-to-come-to-australias-aid-fact-check/5559288.

Ball, Desmond. "The Strategic Essence." *Australian Journal of International Affairs*, vol. 55, no. 2. July 1, 2001.

Baumann, Paul R. "History of Remote Sensing, Satellite Imagery, Part II." Suny Oneta College. 2009. https://www.oneonta.edu/ faculty/baumanpr/geosat2/RS%20 History%20II/RS-History-Part-2.html.

Biddington, Brett. "An Australian Perspective on Space Security." in *Collective Security in Space: Asian Perspectives*, edited by John M. Logsdon and James Clay Moltz. Washington,DC: The George Washington University, The Elliot School of International Affairs, Space Policy Institute, 2008.

Bloomberg Markets. "Company Overview of European Organization for the Exploitation of Meteorological Satellites." Accessed March 1, 2018. https://www.bloomberg.com/research/stocks/private/snapshot.asp? privcapId=8597933.

Brissett, Wilson. "US Allies on the Move in Space." *Air Force Magazine.* October 27, 2017. http://www.airforcemag.com/Features/Pages/2017/October%202017/US-Allies-on-the-Move-in-Space.aspx.

Cheng, Joey. "Stratcom signs space data agreement with U.K., Canada, Australia." Defense Systems. September 23, 2014. https://defensesystems.com/articles/2014/09/23/us-multination-space-agreement.aspx.

Claverie, Alain, Jean-Pierre Darnis, Gil Denis, Xavier Pasco, Murielle Lafaye, Benoît de Maupeou, and Eric Morel. "Towards Disruptions in Earth Observation? New Earth Observation Systems and Markets Evolution: Possible Scenarios and Impacts." *Acta Astronautica*, no. 137. 2017.

Clayton, James. "Japan's Aerospace Industry Takes Off." *The Christian Science Monitor*. January 31, 1990.

CNES. "The Second Biggest Budget in the World." January 6, 2017. https://cnes.fr/fr/web/CNES-fr/11507-le-2eme-budget-au-monde.php [translated by the author].

———. "Fifty Years After Veronique." March 26, 2009. https://cnes.fr/en/web/CNES-fr/7527-les-50-ans-de-veronique.php [translated by the author].

———. "CERES." June 10, 2015. https://ceres.cnes.fr/en/ceres-2.

———. "CNES Facilities." February 18, 2003. https://cnes.fr/en/web/CNES-en/3801-cnes-facilities.php.

———. "CSO/MUSIS." May 30, 2015. https://cso.cnes.fr/en/csomusis-0.

———. "FR-1, CNES' First Satellite in 1965." January 22, 2015. https://www. youtube.com/ watch?v=NIS_ cDyc9PI [translated by the author].

———. "France Celebrates the First 50 Years of its Space Agency." 2011. https://cnes.fr/ sites/default/files/migration/automne/standard/2014_10/p9701_0c600498df91d62 c08ba06c5143f7e0aDP_50_ans_CNES.pdf [translated by the author].

———. "The *Symphonie* Program." Accessed February 16, 2018. http://www.cnes-observatoire.net/actualites/actu2/73_appel-a-projet-symphonie/Symphonie_Synthese_fr.pdf [translated by the author].

Coleman, Matt. "Inside Nurrungar." Australian Broadcasting Corporation. September 16, 1999. http://www.abc.net.au/pm/stories/ s52512.htm.

Commission to Assess U.S. National Security Space Management and Organization. *Report of the Commission to Assess U.S. National Security Space Management and Organization.* January 11, 2001. https://fas.org/spp/military/commission/ report.htm.

Company-Histories.com. "COMSAT Corporation." 1998. http://www. company-histories.com/COMSAT-Corporation-Company-History.html.

Corliss, William R. *Histories of the Space Tracking and Data Acquisition Network (STADAN), the Manned Space Flight Network (MSFN), and the NASA Communications Network (NASCOM).* NASA. June 1974. https://ntrs.nasa.gov/archive/nasa/casi.ntrs.nasa.gov/19750002909.pdf.

Crockett, Barton. "Aussie Gov't Gives Optus Nod to Set Up New Carriers; BellSouth, Cable & Wireless to head up effort." Network World. December 2, 1991.

CSIRO. "About Canberra Deep Space Communications Complex." Accessed March 25, 2018. https://www.csiro.au/en/ResearchFacilities/CDSCC/About-CDSCC.

Culliver, Paul. "50 Years since Australia's First Satellite, WRESAT, launched from Australia." Australian Broadcasting Corporation. November 28, 2017. http://www.abc.net.au/news/2017-11-29/50-years-since-first-satellite-launch-wresat/9205878.

Day, Allison. "Joint Tactical Ground Station Opens at Misawa." Pacific Air Forces. January 23, 2008. http://www.pacaf.af.mil/News/Article-Display/Article 596548/joint-tactical-ground-station-opens-at-misawa/.

Day, Dwayne A. "Ugly little gem: The Teal Ruby Satellite." *The Space Review*. September 14 2015. http://www.thespacereview.com/article/2599/2.

Defense-Aerospace. "Australia-US Joint Facility to Be Hosted at Geraldton." February 15, 2007. http://www. defense-aerospace.com/articles-view/release/3/78992/Australia-agrees-to-host-new-us-satcom-facility.html.

Defense Department and Office of the Director of National Intelligence. *National Security Space Strategy (Unclassified Summary)*. Washington, DC: U.S. Department of Defense. January 2011. http://archive.defense.gov/home/features/2011/0111_nsss/.

Department of Defence. *2016 Defence White Paper*. February 25, 2016. http://www.defence.gov.au/whitepaper/.

———. "About the Woomera Prohibited Area." Accessed March 19, 2018. http://www.defence.gov.au/woomera/about.htm.

———. Defending Australia in the Asia Pacific Century: Force 2030. May 2, 2009. http://www.defence.gov.au/whitepaper/2009/.

———. "DSTO Edinburgh, South Australia." 2017. http://www.defence.gov.au/id/_Master/docs/NCRP/SA/1073DSTOEdinburghSA.pdf.

———. "Defence Project 799." Accessed April 8, 2018. http://www.defence.gov.au/AGO/library/DEF_799_Enhanced_Satellite_ISR_Capability.pdf

———. "Defence Project 799: Enhanced Satellite ISR Capability." Accessed March 24, 2018. http://www.defence.gov.au/AGO/geoint-def799-satellites.htm.

———. *Defence White Paper 2013*. May 3, 2013. http://www.defence. gov.au/whitepaper/2013/.

———. "History." Accessed April 8, 2018. https://www.asd.gov.au/ about/history.htm.

———. "Jindalee Operational Radar Network," Accessed April 6, 2018. https://www.dst.defence.gov.au/innovation/jindalee-operational-radar-network.

———. "MOU Signed for Australia-US Joint Military Communication Ground Station." August 11, 2007. https://archive.is/20121127003933/http:// www.defence.gov.au/media/DepartmentalTpl.cfm?CurrentId=7242#selection-509.59-509.148.

———. "National Security and Intelligence, Surveillance, and Reconnaissance Division: Strategic Plan 2016–2020." August 25, 2016. https://www.dst.defence.gov.au/sites/default/files/divisions/documents/National%20Security%20and%20ISR%20S%26T% 20Strategy%202016-2020.pdf.

Department of the Environment and Energy. "Naval Communication Station Harold E Holt (Area A), Exmouth, WA, Australia." Accessed April 5, 2018, http://www. environment.gov.au/cgi-bin/ahdb/search.pl?mode=place_detail;place_id=103552.

Department of External Affairs. *Security Treaty between Australia, New Zealand and the United States of America [ANZUS]*. September 1, 1951. http://www.austlii.edu. au/au/other/dfat/treaties/1952/2.html.

Department of Foreign Affairs and Trade. "Joint Statement on space security AUSMIN 2010." Accessed April 27, 2018. http://dfat.gov.au/geo/united-states-of-america/ausmin/Pages/joint-statement-on-space-security.aspx.

Department of Industry, Innovation and Science. "The State of Space Report." Accessed March 24, 2018. https://www.industry.gov.au/industry/IndustrySectors/space/Publications/Pages/The-State-of-Space-Report.aspx.

Dolman, Everett C. *Astropolitik: Classical Geopolitics in the Space Age*. London: Frank Cass, 2002.

Elliot, Gene. "Joint Force Tracking Items Orbiting Earth." *Air Force*, vol. 57, no. 9. May 21, 2015. http://www.defence.gov.au/Publications/NewsPapers/Raaf/editions/5709a/5709a.pdf.

———. "Satellite Monitoring System Comes Online in September." *Air Force*, vol. 57, no. 9. May 21, 2015. http://www.defence.gov.au/Publications/NewsPapers/Raaf/editions/5709a/5709a.pdf.

Erwin, Sandra. "Defense Department Turning Over Space Traffic Management to Commerce, but Details still Unclear." *Space News*. May 7, 2018. http://spacenews.com/defense-department-turning-over-space-traffic-management-to-commerce-but-details-still-unclear/.

———. "DoD space policy chief: 'It's imperative that we innovate.'" Space News. December 4, 2017. http://spacenews.com/dod-space-policy-chief-its-imperative-that-we-innovate/.

ESA. "Ariane 6." July 12, 2017. https://www.esa.int/Our_Activities/Space_Transportation/Launch_vehicles/ Ariane_6.

———. "ESA and CNES Sign Contract on CSG." May 2, 2002. http://www.esa.int/Our_Activities/Space_Transportation/ESA_and_CNES_sign_contract_on_CSG.

——— "Europe's Space Port." May 3, 2017. https://www.esa.int/Our_Activities/Space_Transportation/Europe_s_ Spaceport/Europe_s_Spaceport2.

————— "What is Galiléo?." Accessed February 19, 2018. http://www.esa.int/Our_
      Activities/Navigation/Galileo/What_is_Galileo.

EUMETSAT. "Current Satellites." Accessed February 20, 2018. https://www.eumetsat.
      int/website/home/Satellites/CurrentSatellites/index.html.

EU Satellite Centre. *EU Satellite Centre Annual Report 2015*. 2016. https://www.satcen.
      europa.eu/key_documents/EU%20SatCen%20Annual%20Report%202015571e3f
      8bf9d72519a0411205.pdf.

————— *EU Satellite Centre Annual Report 2016*. 2017. https://www.
      satcen.europa.eu/key_documents/EU%20SatCen%20Annual%20Report%202016
      58e24cb1f9d7202538bed52b.pdf.

la Faveur, Sébastien Matte. "The Interest and Opposition of the French Military in
      Satellite Reconnaissance for France: A Talk with a General Officer of the French
      Forces." Space Chronicle vol 59, sup 1. 2006.

Federation of American Scientists. "A Graves Sourcebook." August 7, 2013. https://fas.
      org/spp/military/program/track/graves.pdf.

Foust, Jeff. "Australia to Establish a National Space Agency," *Space News*. September
      24, 2017. http://spacenews.com/australia-to-establish-national-space-agency/.

France Diplomatie. "France's Role in European Space Policy." Accessed March 4, 2018.
      https://www.diplomatie.gouv.fr/en/french-foreign-policy/scientific-
      diplomacy/cooperation-in-the-space-sector/article/france-s-role-in-european-
      space.

George, Roger and Robert Kline. *Intelligence and the National Security Strategist:
      enduring issues and challenges*. Lanham, Md.: Rowman & Littlefield, 2006.

Gosnold, "Hearing of the French Joint Commander for Space." *Satellite Observation*.
      February 5, 2018. https://satelliteobservation.wordpress.com/2018/02/05/hearing-
      of-the-french-joint-commander-for-space/.

GPS.gov. "Joint Announcement on Japan-United States GPS Cooperation." July 24,
      2013. https://www.gps.gov/policy/cooperation/japan/2013-joint-announcement/.

Graham, William. "Japanese H-IIA Launches IGS Optical 6 Satellite." *NASA
      Spaceflight.com*. February 26, 2018. https://www.nasaspaceflight.com/2018/02/
      japanese-h-iia-rocket-igs-6-launch/.

Gruss, Mike. "U.S., France Expand Data-sharing Agreement." SpaceNews. April 16,
      2015. http://spacenews.com/us-france-expand-space-data-sharing-agreement/.

Hays, Peter. "The Military Use of Space: A diagnostic Assessment / On the Edge of ...." *Air and Space Power Journal*, vol. 16, no. 3. Fall 2002.

Heisbourg, Francois and Xavier Pasco, *Espace Militaire: L'Europe entre souveraineté et cooperation.* Paris: Choiseul, 2011.

Henry, Caleb. "Ariane 5 down to two dozen launches before Ariane 6 takes over." SpaceNews. January 16, 2018. *Space News.* http://spacenews.com/ariane-5-down-to-two-dozen-launches-before-ariane-6-takes-over/.

———. "Australian Military Frustrated by Out of Sync Space and Ground Assets." *Space News.* July 3, 2017. http://spacenews.com/australian-military-frustrated-by-out-of-sync-space-and-ground-assets/.

———. "Australia's Military Including Commercial Capacity in Its Satellite Communications Plan." *Space News.* May 22, 2017. http://spacenews.com/australias-military-including-commercial-capacity-in-its-satellite-communications-plans/.

———. "French DGA Orders Two All-Electric Military Satellites as Syracuse III Sucessor." *Via Satellite.* December 23, 2015. http://www.satellitetoday.com/government-military/2015/12/23/french-dga-orders-two-all-electric-military-satellites-as-Syracuse-3-successor/undefined.

Hitchens, Theresa and Joan Johnson-Freese. "Toward a New National Security Strategy: Time for Strategic Rebalancing." Atlantic Council Strategy Paper no. 5, Atlantic Council. June 2016.

Howell, Elizabeth. "Tanegashima: Japan's Largest Space Center," *Space.com.* September 30, 2016. https://www.space.com/34270-tanegashima-space-center.html.

Hubbard, Christopher. *Australian and U.S. Military Cooperation: Fighting Common Enemies.* Hampshire, UK and Burlington, VT: Ashgate, 2005.

Hughes, Christopher. "Japan, Ballistic Missile Defence and Remilitarisation." *Space Policy.* April 2, 2013. http://dx.doi.org/10.1016/j.spacepol.2013.03.004.

International Astronautical Federation. "Space Coordination Office, Department of Industry." Accessed March 24, 2018. http://www. iafastro.org/societes/space-coordination-office-department-of-industry/.

International Institute for Strategic Studies. "The Emerging European Military Space Capability." *Strategic Comments*, vol. 2, No. 3. 1996. https://doi.org/10.1080/1356788960233.

Irsten, Gabriella. "The Consultation Process for the International Code of Conduct for Outer Space Activities Ends." Reaching Critical Will. Accessed February 25, 2018. http://reachingcriticalwill.org/news/ latest-news/8907-the-consultation-process-for-the-international-code-of-conduct-for-outer-space-activities-ends.

Japan Meteorological Agency. "Meteorological Satellites -Japan Meteorological Agency (JMA)-." Accessed May 6, 2018. http://www.jma.go.jp/jma/jma-eng/satellite/.

Japanese Ministry of Defense. *The Guidelines for Japan-U.S. Defense Cooperation.* April 27, 2015. http://www.mod.go.jp/e/d_act/anpo/shishin_20150427e.html.

JAXA. "Advanced Optical Satellite (ALOS-3)." Accessed May 5, 2018. http://global.jaxa.jp/projects/sat/alos3/.

———. "Overview of the Tracking and Control Center at the Tsukuba Space Center." Accessed May 12, 2018. http://www.jaxa.jp/countdown/f11/presskit/kiku8_ tracking_e.pdf.

———. "Space Transportation Systems." Accessed May 6, 2018. http://global.jaxa.jp/ projects/rockets/.

Johnson-Freese, Joan. *Space as a Strategic Asset.* New York: Columbia University Press, 2007.

Johnson, Chris. "Draft International Code of Conduct for Outer Space Activities Fact Sheet." Secure World Foundation. February 2015. https://swfound.org/media/ 166384/swf_draft_international_code_of_conduct_for_outer_space_activities_fac t_sheet_february_2014.pdf.

Kallender, Paul. "Japan's New Dual-Use Space Policy: The Long Road to the 21st Century." Institut Français des Relations Internationales. November 2016.

Kallender-Umezu, Paul. "A New Direction for Japan's Space Program?" *Aviation Week and Space Technology.* May 6, 2013.

———. "Profile | Hiroshi Imazu, Former Chairman, Space Policy Committee, Liberal Democratic Party of Japan." *Space News.* October 27, 2014. spacenews.com/42331profile-hiroshi-imazu-former-chairman-space-policy-committee-liberal/.

Kenyon, Henry S. "Spacecraft Ties Distant Battlefields into One Network." *Signal.* September 2003. https://www.afcea.org/content/?q=node/155.

Klein, John J. *Space Warfare: Strategy, Principles, and Policy.* New York: Routledge, 2006.

Klinkrad, H. "Monitoring Space – Efforts Made by European Countries." Accessed March 1, 2018. http://www.fas.org/spp/military/program/track/klinkrad.pdf.

Kotecki, Steve. "C-band Radar Reaches Full Operational Capability in Australia." *Peterson Space Observer*. March 7, 2017. http://www.csmng.com/2017/03/17/c-band-radar-reaches-full-operational-capability-in-australia/

Krebs, Gunter Dirk. "DSN 1 / Superbird 8 (Kirameki 1 / Superbird B3)." Accessed May 12, 2018. http://space.skyrocket.de/doc_sdat/dsn-1_superbird-8.htm.

———. "MOS 1a, 1b (Momo 1a, 1b)." *Gunter's Space Page*. Accessed April 27, 2018. http://space.skyrocket.de/doc_sdat/mos.htm.

———. "Télécom 1A, 1B, 1C," *Gunter's Space Page*. Accessed March 11, 2018. http://space.skyrocket.de/doc_sdat/telecom-1.htm.

———. "Wresat," *Gunter's Space Page*. Accessed March 19, 2018. http://space.skyrocket.de/doc_sdat/wresat.htm.

Krige, John. In *Science and Technology in the Global Cold War*, edited by Naomi Oreskes. Cambridge, Mass.: The MIT Press, 2014.

Krige, John, Angelina Long Cahhahan, and Ashok Mahara. *NASA in the World: Fifty Years of International Collaboration in Space*. New York: Palgrave Macmillan, 2013.

Kruse, Richard. "Japanese Launch Vehicles." *Historic Spacecraft*. Accessed May 3, 2018. http://historicspacecraft.com/Rockets_Japanese.html.

Lepage, Andrew J. "Old Reliable: The Story of the Redstone." The Space Review. May 2, 2011. http://www.thespacereview.com/article/1836/1.

Leslie, Tim and Mark Corcoran. "Explained: Australia's Involvement with the NSA, the U.S. Spy Agency at the Heart of the Global Scandal." Australia Broadcasting Corporation. November 18, 2013. http://www.abc.net.au/news/ 2013–11-08/australian-nsa-involvement-explained/5079786.

Liff, Adam P. "Policy by Other Means: Collective Self-Defense and the Politics of Japan's Postwar Constitutional Reinterpretations." *Asia Policy*, no. 24. July 2017. https://doi.org/10.1353/asp.2017.0035.

Liou, J. C. "Growth of Orbital Debris," 4th ASEAN Regional Forum (ARF) Workshop on Space Security. October 24–25, 2016. https://ntrs.nasa.gov/archive/nasa/casi.ntrs.nasa.gov/20160012733.pdf.

Lowman, Paul D., Jr.. "Geologic Orbital Photography: Experience from the Gemini Program." June 1968. https://ntrs.nasa.gov/archive/nasa/casi.ntrs.nasa.gov/ 19680018143.pdf.

Lutes, Charles D. and Peter Hays. *Toward a Theory of Spacepower: Selected Essays.* Washington, DC: National Defense University, 2011.

MacDonald, Fraser. "Anti-Astropolitik – outer space and the orbit of geography." *Progress in Human Geography*, vol. 31, no. 5. 2007.

Mallet, Jean-Claude. *Défense et Sécurité nationale: le Livre blanc.* June 2008. http://www.ladocumentation francaise.fr/var/storage/rapports-publics/084000341.pdf.

Mariquez, Manuel. "Japan's Space Law Revision: the Next Step toward Re-Militarization?" Nuclear Threat Initiative. January 1, 2008. http://www.nti.org/analysis/articles/japans-space-law-revision/.

Matsuura, Mayumi. In "Preventing Collisions between Debris and Spacecraft" by Doug Messier. *Parabolic Arc.* May 9, 2017. http://www.parabolicarc.com/2017/ 05/09/preventing-collisions-between-debris-spacecraft/.

Meyer, Paul. "Dark forces awaken: the prospects for cooperative space security." *The Nonproliferation Review,* vol. 23, nos. 3–4. June-July 2016. DOI: 10.1080/ 10736700.2016.1268750.

Ministère des Armées. "The Joint Space Command." March 26, 2012. https://www.defense.gouv .fr/actualites/dossiers/l-espace-au-profit-des-operations-militaires/fiches-techniques/cie [translated by the author].

———. "The Space Surveillance Division of the Air Defense and Air Operations Command." March 20, 2012. https://www.defense.gouv.fr/english/ actualites/dossiers/l-espace-au-profit-des-operations-militaires/fiches-techniques/dse-cdaoa [translated by the author].

———. *Revue Stratégique de défense et de sécurité nationale.* October 13, 2017. https://www.defense.gouv.fr/dgris/politique-de-defense/revue-strategique/revue-strategique.

Ministry of Defense. "The Guidelines for Japan-U.S. Defense Cooperation." April 27, 2015. http://www.mod.go.jp/e/d_act/anpo/shishin_20150427e.html.

Moltz, James Clay. *Asia's Space Race: National Motivations, Regional Rivalries, and International Risks.* New York: Columbia University Press, 2011.

———. "Coalitions in Space: Where Networks Are Power." *Space and Defense*, vol. 5, no. 1. Summer 2011.

————. "Next Steps yowards Space Security," in *Space Security*, edited by Sukhvinder Kaur Multani. India: The Ifcai University Press, 2008.

NY2O.com. "DSN-2." Accessed May 12, 2018. https://www.n2yo.com/?s=41940&live =1.

————. "Geostationary Satellites." N2YO.com - Real Time Satellite Tracking and Predictions. Accessed February 28, 2018. https://n2yo.com/satellites /?c=10.

————. "Military Satellites." Accessed April 27, 2018. http://www.n2yo.com/ satellites/?c=30&srt=1&dir=1.

NASA. "Aeronautics and Space Report of the President: Department of Defense (DoD)." 1997. https://history.nasa.gov/presrp97/dod.htm.

————. "FR1." March 21, 2017. https://nssdc.gsfc.nasa.gov/nmc/spacecraftDisplay. do?id=1965-101A.

The National Archives. "The Blue Streak Rocket." Accessed March 19, 2018. http:// www.nationalarchives.gov.uk/films/1951to1964/filmpage _rocket.htm.

National Archives of Australia. "Defence Research and the Anglo-Australian Joint Project." Accessed March 19, 2018. http://guides.naa.gov .au/records-about-south-australia/chapter15/15.4.aspx.

National Library of Australia. "Weapons Research Establishment (Australia) (1955-1978)." Accessed March 19, 2018. https://trove.nla.gov .au/people/783674.

National Oceanic and Atmospheric Administration. "International Partners in the Sky: Satellite Partnerships." February 12, 2018. https://www.nesdis.noaa.gov/content/ international-partners-sky-satellite-partnerships.

National Security Agency. "Appendices to U.S. – British Communication Intelligence Agreement." March 5, 1946. https://www.nsa.gov/news-features/declassified-documents/ukusa/assets/files/ appendices_ jul48.pdf.

———— "UKUSA Agreement Release: 1940–1956." June 24, 2010. https://www.nsagov/news-features/declassified-documents/ukusa/.

National Space Policy Secretariat. "Implementation Plan of the Basic Plan on Space Policy." December 17, 2017. http://www8.cao.go.jp/space/english/basicplan/ 2017/basicplan.pdf.

————. "[Movie] Quasi-Zenith Satellite System 'QZSS'." December 3, 2016. http://qzss.go.jp/en/overview/downloads/movie_qzss.html.

———. "Quasi-Zenith Satellite System." March 11, 2018. https://web.archive.org/web/20180311021244/http://qzss.go.jp/en/overview/notices/service_180302.html.

O'Connell, James. "Memorandum Concerning U.S Assistance in the Development of Foreign Communications Satellite Capabilities." September 17, 1965. In *Exploring the Unknown: Select Documents in the History of the U.S. Civilian Space Program*, vol. 3, edited by John M. Logsdon. Washington, DC: NASA, 1998.

Office of the Assistant Secretary of Defense for Homeland Defense. *Department of Defense International Space Cooperation Strategy*. January 1, 2017. http://www.dtic.mil/dtic/tr/fulltext/u2/1034871.pdf.

Office of National Space Policy. "New 'Basic Plan on Space Policy' (Tentative Translation, January 16th, 2015)." January 16, 2015. http://aerospace-wpengine.netdna-ssl.com/wpcontent/uploads/2018/04/Japan-Basic-Plan-9Jan15.pdf [translated by Aerospace].

Office of the President of the United States. *National Security Strategy of the United States of America*. December 2017.

———. *National Space Transportation Policy*. November 21, 2013. https://obamawhitehouse.archives.gov/sites/default/files/microsites/ostp/national_space_transportation_policy_11212013.pdf.

Parliament of Australia. "Project JP 3029 Phase 2 – Defence Space Surveillance Telescope Facilities Project." September 2014. http://www.aph.gov.au/~/media/02%20Parliamentary%20Business/ 24%20Committees/244%20Joint%20Committees/PWC/Report%207-2014/Chapter%202. pdf?l=en.

Pekkanen, Saadia M. and Paul Kallender-Umezu. *In Defense of Japan: From the Market to the Military in Space Policy*. Stanford, CA: Stanford University Press, 2010.

Pellerin, Cheryl. "DARPA to Transfer Advanced Space Debris Telescope to Air Force." U.S. Department of Defense. October 18, 2016. https://www.defense.gov/News/Article/Article/976146/darpa-to-transfer-advanced-space-debris-telescope-to-air-force/.

Phys.org. "Australian Satellite in Orbit." May 26, 2017. https://phys.org/news/2017-05-australian-satellite-orbit.html.

Prime Minister's Office. *National Security Strategy 2013* (provisional translation). December 17, 2013. http://japan.kantei.go.jp/96_abe/documents/2013/__icsFiles/afieldfile/2013/12/17/NSS.pdf.

Radcliffe, William W. "Origins and Current State of Japan's Reconnaissance Satellite Program (U)." *Studies in Intelligence*, vol. 54, no. 3. September 2010.

Richelson, Jeffrey T. *America's Space Sentinels: DSP Satellites and National Security.* Lawrence, Kansas: University of Kansas Press, 1999.

Robinson, Jana. "Space Security through the Transatlantic Partnership." Space Policy, no. 28. February 1, 2012.

Sawako, Maeda. "Transformation of Japanese Space Policy: From the 'Peaceful Use of space' to the 'Basic Law on Space'." *The Asia-Pacific Journal,* vol. 7, no. 1. November 2, 2009.

Scott, Alan D. "Coalition Building in Space: Initial Technical Considerations and Potential Implementation Strategies." Prepared as a supplement to the Defense Threat Reduction Agency's project on "Allied Security and an Integrated Satellite Network." August 2011.

Sebesta, Lorenza. "Chapter 11, U.S.-European Relations and the Decision to Build Ariane, the European Launch Vehicle." In *SP-4217 Beyond the Ionosphere,* edited by Andrew Butrica. January 21, 2013. https://history.nasa.gov/SP-4217/ch11.htm.

de Selding, Peter B. "Ariane-5 Lofts Athena-Fidus and ABS's First Built to Order Satellite." *Space News.* February 7, 2014. http://spacenews.com/39410ariane-5-lofts-athena-fidus-and-abss-1st-built-to-order-satellite/.

————. "French Spirale Satellites to Continue Mission-detection Test Mission thru End of Year." *Space News.* June 21, 2010. http://spacenews.com/ french-spirale-satellites-continue-missile-detection-test-mission-through-end-year/.

————. "U.S., Japan Pledge Closer Cooperation on Space Surveillance." *Space News.* October 4, 2013. http://spacenews.com/37551us-japan-pledge-closer-cooperation-on-space-surveillance/.

Sheehan, Michael. "Chapter 5: European Integration and Space." In *The International Politics of Space.* New York: Routledge, 2007.

Sheldon, John B. "Astropolitik: Classical Geopolitics in the Space Age," *Comparative Strategy,* vol. 21, no. 3. 2002.

Singtel Optus Pty Limited. "Optus C1: An Australian Hotbird." Accessed April 8, 2018. https://www.optus.com.au/about/ network/satellite/fleet/c1.

Skybrokers. "Singtel Optus Australia." Accessed April 6, 2018. http://www.sky-brokers.com/home/services/satelite-operators/singtel-optus-australia.

SKY Perfect JSAT. "Superbird-C2." Accessed May 12, 2018. http://www.jsat.net/en/ contour/superbird-c2.html.

Spaceflight 101.com. "DSN-2 Satellite." Accessed May 12, 2018. https://spaceflight101. com/h-iia-dsn-2/dsn-2/.

———. "Quasi-Zenith Satellite System." Accessed May 6, 2018. http://spaceflight101.com/spacecraft/qzss/.

Space Launch Report. "Ariane 5 Data Sheet." *Space Launch Report.* Accessed January 25, 2018. http://www.spacelaunchreport.com/ariane5.html.

Space News Editor. "Missile Warning Data System Ordered for Australia." *Space News.* September 30, 2013. http://spacenews.com/37458missile-warning-data-system-ordered-for-australia/.

———. "U.S. Putting Space-tracking Radar, Telescope in Australia." *Space News.* November 16, 2012. http://spacenews.com/us-putting-space-tracking-radar-telescope-in-australia/.

Space News Staff. "French Joint Space Command on Schedule to Open in July." *Space News.* April 25, 2010. http://spacenews.com/french-joint-space-command-schedule-open-july/.

Standing Committee on Economics. *Lost in Space? Setting a new direction for Australia's space science and industry sector.* The Parliament of the Commonwealth of Australia. November 12, 2008. https://www.aph.gov.au/ Parliamentary_Business/Committees/Senate/Economics/Completed_inquiries/200 8-10/space_08/report/ index.

Standing Committee on Public Works. "RAAF Base Edinburgh, Redevelopment Stage 1, Adelaide." The Parliament of the Commonwealth of Australia. October 5, 2000. aph.gov.au.

Stone, Christopher. "Security through Vulnerability? The False Deterrence of the National Security Space Strategy," *The Space Review.* April 13, 2015. http://www.thespacereview.com/article/2731/1.

Suzuki, Kazuto. "Transforming Japan's Space Policy-Making." *Space Policy*, vol. 23. April 2, 2007. doi: 10.1016/j.spacepol.2007.02.001.

Svitak, Amy. "EU aims for Space Situational Awareness Network," *Aviation Week.* August 5, 2013. http:// aviationweek.com/awin/eu-aims-space-situational-awareness-network.

Svitak, Amy. "U.S. Electronics Firm Fined $8 million for Export Violations: As U.S. Loosens Satellite Export Rules, Suppliers Own Up to Violations." *Aviation Week*. September 16, 2013. http://aviationweek.com/awin/us-electronics-firm-fined-8-million-export-violations.

The Tauri Group, *State of the Satellite Industry Report*, September 2015, https://www.sia. org/wp-content/uploads/2015/06/Mktg15-SSIR-2015-FINAL-Compressed.pdf.

Telespazio. "Sicral 2." Accessed February 19, 2018. www.telespazio.com/documents/ 9986169/43239100/SICRAL2_scheda_eng.pdf.

Television.au. "Aussat: Dawn of TV's Satellite Age." August 27, 2015. http:// televisionau.com/2015/08/aussat-dawn-of-tvs-satellite-age.html.

Testé, Jean-Daniel. "SSA: first priority of French military space policy 2025." March 2015. www.jsforum.or.jp/stableuse/2016/pdf/15.%20Teste.pdf.

Thales Group. "Syracuse II: Satellite Communications Leveraging Joint C4ISR Capabilities." Accessed February 19, 2018. https://www.thalesgroup.com/sites/ default/files/asset/document/Syracuse_gb.pdf.

Tsaio, Sunny. *Read You Loud and Clear! : The Story of NASA's Tracing and Data Flight Network*. NASA. 2008. https://ntrs.nasa.gov/search.jsp?R=20080020389.

Trask, Steven. "Government Announces Creation of National Space Agency." The Canberra Times. September 26, 2017. http://www.canberratimes.com.au/ technology/sci-tech/government-announces-creation-of-national-space-agency-20170924-gynx 3c.html?_ga=2.235353091.385887290.1521838567-1793460573.1521838567.

United States Air Force. "1 RSU Space Systems." January 25, 2017. http://www. peterson.af.mil/ About/Fact-Sheets/Display/Article/1059617/1-rsu-space-systems/.

United States Army. "MDSS Project Office." Accessed April 28, 2018. https://www.msl. army.mil/Pages/mdss/jtags.html.

United States Congress. *National Defense Authorization Act for Fiscal Year 2000*. Public Law 106–65, 106th Cong., 1st sess. January 6, 1999.

United States Department of State. "Joint Statement: The Fourth Meeting of the U.S.-Japan Comprehensive Dialogue on Space." May 17, 2017. https://www.state. gov/r/pa/prs/ps/2017/05/270946.htm.

United States Geological Survey. "Earth Resources Observation Satellite (EROS) Program." https://eros.usgs.gov/sites/all/files/external/eros/history/1970s/ Documents/1966-1977_Earth_Resources_Observation_Systems %28EROS %29_Program.pdf.

United States Government. *Security Treaty between the United States and Japan; September 8, 1951.* September 8, 1951. http://avalon.law.yale.edu/20th_century/ japan001.asp#1.

———. *Treaty of Mutual Cooperation and Security between the United States of America and Japan.* January 19, 1960. http://afe.easia.columbia. edu/ps/japan/mutual_cooperation_ treaty.pdf.

United States Strategic Command Public Affairs. "USSTRATCOM Hosts Space Exercise with International Partners." October 3, 2016. http://www.stratcom.mil/Media/ News/News-Article-View/Article/984307/usstratcom-hosts-space-exercise-with-international-partners/.

Vasquez, Arielle. "WGS-9 satellite launches from Florida." U.S. Air Force. March 29, 2017. http://www.schriever.af.mil/News/Article-Display/Article/1134074/wgs-9-satellite-launches-from-florida/.

Werner, Debra. "International SSA Agreements Could Pave the Way for Further Space Cooperation, Panelists Said." *Space News.* April 18, 2018. http://spacenews. com/international-ssa-agreements-could-pave-the-way-for-further-space-cooperation-panelists-said/.

Yamamoto, Shizuo. "Overview of JAXA Activities on Sustainable Space Development and Space Situational Awareness." JAXA. February 26, 2015. http://www. jsforum.or.jp/debrisympo/2015/pdf/09S2DS2A2015_JAXA_KNote_0225.pdf.

INITIAL DISTRIBUTION LIST

1.   Defense Technical Information Center
     Ft. Belvoir, Virginia

2.   Dudley Knox Library
     Naval Postgraduate School
     Monterey, California

www.ingramcontent.com/pod-product-compliance
Lightning Source LLC
Chambersburg PA
CBHW050620110426

42813CB00010B/2618